BUILDING VOCABULARY
SKILLS & STRATEGIES

LEVEL 7

by **EMILY HUTCHINSON**

BUILDING VOCABULARY
SKILLS & STRATEGIES

LEVEL **3**
LEVEL **4**
LEVEL **5**
LEVEL **6**
LEVEL **7** ⇦
LEVEL **8**

Development and Production: Laurel Associates, Inc.
Cover Design: Image Quest, Inc.

SADDLEBACK
PUBLISHING·INC.
Three Watson
Irvine, CA 92618-2767

E-Mail: info@sdlback.com
Website: www.sdlback.com

Copyright © 2004 by Saddleback Publishing, Inc. All rights reserved. No part of this book may be reproduced in any form or by any means, electronic or mechanical, including photocopying, recording, or by any information storage and retrieval system, without the written permission of the publisher, with the exception below.

Pages labeled with the statement **Saddleback Publishing, Inc. © 2004** are intended for reproduction. Saddleback Publishing, Inc. grants to individual purchasers of this book the right to make sufficient copies of reproducible pages for use by all students of a single teacher. This permission is limited to a single teacher, and does not apply to entire schools or school systems.

ISBN 1-56254-725-9

Printed in the United States of America
10 09 08 07 06 05 04   9 8 7 6 5 4 3 2 1

CONTENTS

Introduction .5

English Vocabularies: Formal, Informal,
   and Slang 1 6

English Vocabularies: Formal, Informal,
   and Slang 2 7

Using the Dictionary 1 8

Using the Dictionary 2 9

Information in a Dictionary Entry 1 10

Information in a Dictionary Entry 2 11

Denotation and Connotation 1 12

Denotation and Connotation 2 13

Just for Fun: Dictionary Challenge 1 . . .14

Just for Fun: Dictionary Challenge 2 . . .15

Pronunciation: Vowel Sounds 1 16

Pronunciation: Vowel Sounds 2 17

Pronunciation: Silent Letters 1 18

Pronunciation: Silent Letters 2 19

Pronunciation: Syllables and
   Accent Marks 1 20

Pronunciation: Syllables and
   Accent Marks 2 21

Using Context Clues 1 22

Using Context Clues 2 23

Nouns: Getting Meaning from
   Context Clues 24

Verbs: Getting Meaning from
   Context Clues 25

Adjectives: Getting Meaning
   from Context Clues 26

Adverbs: Getting Meaning from
   Context Clues 27

Forms of a Word: Adjective to Noun 1 . .28

Forms of a Word: Adjective to Noun 2 . .29

Forms of a Word: Verb to Adjective 1 . . .30

Forms of a Word: Verb to Adjective 2 . . .31

Forms of a Word: Noun to Verb 1 32

Forms of a Word: Noun to Verb 2 33

Just for Fun: Word Ladders 1 34

Just for Fun: Word Ladders 2 35

Making Compound Words 1 36

Making Compound Words 2 37

Compound Words: *Head* and *Foot* 1 . . .38

Compound Words: *Head* and *Foot* 2 . . .39

Compound Words: *Air* and *Water* 1 40

Compound Words: *Air* and *Water* 2 41

Compound Words: *Sun* and *Wind* 1 42

Compound Words: *Sun* and *Wind* 2 43

Choosing Precise Words 1 44

Choosing Precise Words 2 45

Greek Roots 1 46

Greek Roots 2 47

Latin Roots 1 48

Latin Roots 2 49

Prefixes 1 .50

Prefixes 2 .51

Suffixes 1 .52

Suffixes 2 .53

Near Misses 1 54

Near Misses 2 55

Synonyms: Nouns 1 56

Synonyms: Nouns 2 57

Synonyms: Verbs 1 58

Synonyms: Verbs 2 59

Synonyms: Adjectives 1 60

Synonyms: Adjectives 2 61

Synonyms: Adverbs 1 62

Synonyms: Adverbs 2 63

Antonyms: Nouns 1 64

Antonyms: Nouns 2 65

Antonyms: Verbs 1 66

Antonyms: Verbs 2 67

Antonyms: Adjectives 1 68

Antonyms: Adjectives 2 69

Antonyms: Adverbs 1 70

Antonyms: Adverbs 2 71

Homophones 72

Homophone Riddles 73

Homographs 74

Homophones and Homographs:
   Dictionary Practice 75

Clipped Words 1 76	S-T Words in Context 1 108
Clipped Words 2 77	S-T Words in Context 2 109
Words Borrowed from Names 1 78	U-V Words in Context 1 110
Words Borrowed from Names 2 79	U-V Words in Context 2 111
Foreign Words and Phrases 1 80	W-X Words in Context 1 112
Foreign Words and Phrases 2 81	W-X Words in Context 2 113
Simple Idioms 1 82	Y-Z Words in Context 1 114
Simple Idioms 2 83	Y-Z Words in Context 2 115
Interpreting Idioms 1 84	Just for Fun: Explaining Why
Interpreting Idioms 2 85	or Why Not 116
Explaining Idioms 1 86	Just for Fun: Exploring Big Words 117
Explaining Idioms 2 87	Shopping Words 1 118
Using Idioms in Context 1 88	Shopping Words 2 119
Using Idioms in Context 2 89	Law Words 1 120
A-B Words in Context 1 90	Law Words 2 121
A-B Words in Context 2 91	Building Words 1 122
C-D Words in Context 1 92	Building Words 2 123
C-D Words in Context 2 93	Space Words 1 124
E-F Words in Context 1 94	Space Words 2 125
E-F Words in Context 2 95	Health Words 1 126
G-H Words in Context 1 96	Health Words 2 127
G-H Words in Context 2 97	Business Words 1 128
I-J Words in Context 1 98	Business Words 2 129
I-J Words in Context 2 99	Travel Words 1 130
K-L Words in Context 1 100	Travel Words 2 131
K-L Words in Context 2 101	Government Words 1 132
M-N Words in Context 1 102	Government Words 2 133
M-N Words in Context 2 103	Party Words 1 134
O-P Words in Context 1 104	Party Words 2 135
O-P Words in Context 2 105	Scope and Sequence 136
Q-R Words in Context 1 106	Answer Key 138
Q-R Words in Context 2 107	

INTRODUCTION

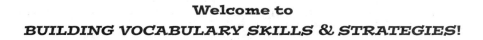

Welcome to BUILDING VOCABULARY SKILLS & STRATEGIES!

We at Saddleback Publishing, Inc. are proud to introduce this important supplement to your basal language arts curriculum. Our goal in creating this series was twofold: to help on-level and below-level students build their "word power" in short incremental lessons, and to provide you, the teacher, with maximum flexibility in deciding when and how to assign these exercises.

All lessons are reproducible. That makes them ideal for homework, extra credit assignments, cooperative learning groups, or focused drill practice for selected ESL or remedial students. A quick review of the book's Table of Contents will enable you to individualize instruction according to the varied needs of your students.

Correlated to the latest research and current language arts standards in most states, the instructional design of *Building Vocabulary Skills & Strategies* is unusually comprehensive for a supplementary program. All important concepts—ranging from primary-level phonics to the nuances of connotation—are thoroughly presented from the ground up. Traditional word attack strategies and "getting meaning from context clues" are dually emphasized.

As all educators know, assessment and evaluation of student understanding and skill attainment is an ongoing process. Here again, reproducible lessons are ideal in that they can be used for both pre- and post-testing. We further suggest that you utilize the blank back of every copied worksheet for extra reinforcement of that lesson's vocabulary; spelling tests or short writing assignments are two obvious options. You can use the Scope and Sequence chart at the back of each book for recording your ongoing evaluations.

ENGLISH VOCABULARIES: FORMAL, INFORMAL, AND SLANG 1

Various occasions call for various kinds of language.

A. Directions: Where will you usually see and hear the *formal* words in the box? In official documents and reports, literary works, and speeches. Use a dictionary to look up any words you don't know. Then write each word next to the *informal* word below that has the same meaning.

| abolish | baffle | calculate | massive | notable |
| perceive | perturb | quest | signify | tedious |

1. **understand** _____
2. **figure** _____
3. **ban** _____
4. **mean** _____
5. **bother** _____
6. **huge** _____
7. **confuse** _____
8. **famous** _____
9. **boring** _____
10. **search** _____

B. Directions: The informal word in each sentence appears in **boldface**. Circle a letter to identify the formal word that could replace it.

1. At the sight of the brightly colored balloons, the child broke into a **sudden** smile.
   a. relevant   b. spontaneous   c. delirious

2. The archaeologists became very excited when they saw the **writing** on the walls of the tomb.
   a. trophy   b. portrayal   c. inscription

3. The hikers were surprised to find that a huge boulder **barred** their path.
   a. obstructed   b. prevailed   c. divulged

4. The detectives thought that the suspect's story was probably a **lie**.
   a. falsehood   b. misdemeanor   c. felony

5. When Melanie slipped and fell on the ice, she **broke** her arm.
   a. sprained   b. injured   c. fractured

Name: _____   **Date:** _____

INFORMATION IN A DICTIONARY ENTRY 2

A. Directions: Some words have more than one acceptable spelling. Remember that the preferred spelling is always listed *first* in a dictionary entry. Complete the word pairs below with either the preferred spelling or its less common alternate.

1. _____ / omelette
2. octopuses / _____
3. _____ / larvas
4. _____ / teepee
5. leveled / _____

6. gladioluses / _____
7. _____ / make-up
8. hallelujah / _____

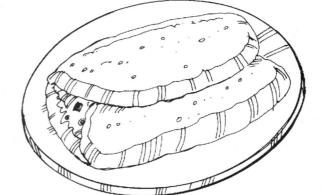

B. Directions:
Some dictionaries include a word's *etymology*, or original source, before or after its definition. Draw a line to match each word with its origin.

1. **anemone**   a. from the Irish word *seamrog*, meaning "little clover"

2. **castanets**   b. named by Spanish dancers who saw that this instrument looked like two chestnuts

3. **catamaran**   c. from two Latin words, *unum* ("one") and *cornu* ("horn")

4. **geranium**   d. from the Tamil word *katta-marran*, meaning "tied wood"

5. **mercurial**   e. from two Greek words, *anemos* ("wind") and *mone* ("habitation")

6. **shamrock**   f. from *Mercury*, the fast messenger of the Roman gods

7. **unicorn**   g. named for the crane, *geranos* in Greek, because its seed pods look like a crane's head

Name: _____   Date: _____

DENOTATION AND CONNOTATION 1

A word's *denotation* is its literal meaning. The *connotation* of the same word may be something quite different.

A word's *connotation* is its implied meaning. Connotation arises from the ideas, emotions, and experiences associated with the word. Two words with nearly the same denotation may have very different connotations.

EXAMPLE:

opponent (positive connotation, suggesting a worthy competitor)

foe (negative connotation, suggesting an enemy)

A. Directions: Write **P** for *positive* or **N** for *negative* next to each word below.

1. ____ wretched
2. ____ unique
3. ____ survive
4. ____ gangster
5. ____ humane
6. ____ sneaky
7. ____ spry
8. ____ embarrass
9. ____ fantastic
10. ____ snob
11. ____ valiant
12. ____ wilt

B. Directions: Words in the box are *synonyms* (with different connotations) of the words below. Write the matching word from the box next to each word below. Hint: You will *not* use all the words.

| accumulate | custodian | devise | aroma | assertive | vigorous |
| bold | crowd | emphasize | doubtful | thin | persuade |

1. contrive / _____
2. aggressive / _____
3. mob / _____
4. hoard / _____
5. brainwash / _____
6. brazen / _____
7. janitor / _____
8. odor / _____
9. belabor / _____
10. gaunt / _____

Name: _____ Date: _____

DENOTATION AND CONNOTATION 2

Making careful word choices ensures that you get your message across.

People use *euphemisms* to replace words that are thought to be too strong or unpleasant.
EXAMPLE: *passed away* instead of *died*

Dysphemisms are harsher words deliberately used to replace neutral words.
EXAMPLE: *quack* instead of *doctor*

Directions: Complete the chart below with the euphemisms, dysphemisms, or neutral words from the box on the right. Hint: You will *not* use all the words.

EUPHEMISM	NEUTRAL WORD	DYSPHEMISM
1. firm	obstinate	_____
2. fervent	_____	hysterical
3. _____	charity	handout
4. move on	leave	_____
5. assist	_____	abet
6. _____	unusual	abnormal
7. developing country	underdeveloped country	_____
8. challenged	_____	crippled
9. _____	worker	hireling
10. peacekeeper	_____	mercenary
11. man's best friend	dog	_____
12. _____	house	shack
13. lounge	_____	toilet

WORD LIST
abandon
abrupt
cur
diner
disabled
donation
emotional
employee
hash-house
help
mansion
pig-headed
quick
restaurant
restroom
rude
soldier
special
third-world

Name: _____ Date: _____

JUST FOR FUN: DICTIONARY CHALLENGE 1

Here's a chance to have some fun with some interesting and unusual words.

Directions: To answer the questions, study the dictionary definitions of the **boldface** words.

1. Would you use the word **redolent** or **refulgent** to describe a **pelargonium**? Explain your answer.

   _____

   _____

   _____

2. In what countries would you find **Qishm** and **Qiqihar**?

   _____

   _____

3. Would you rather have a voice that's **mellifluous** or **cacophonous**? Why?

   _____

   _____

4. Would you go to a **boutique** to buy some **borscht**? Why or why not?

   _____

   _____

5. Would the words **precursors**, **originators**, and **forebears** be used to describe your **progenitors** or your **progeny**? Explain your answer.

   _____

   _____

6. Who would make a better dinner companion—a **gourmand** or an **epicure**? Why?

   _____

   _____

7. Suppose you were in danger. Would you rather have someone **ameliorate** your situation or **exacerbate** it?

   _____

   _____

Name: _____ **Date:** _____

14 *Building Vocabulary Skills and Strategies, Level 7* • Saddleback Publishing, Inc. ©2004 • 3 Watson, Irvine, CA 92618 • Phone (888) SDL-BACK • www.sdlback.com

JUST FOR FUN: DICTIONARY CHALLENGE 2

Directions: To answer the questions, look up the dictionary definitions of the **boldface** words.

1. Would someone deliver a **eulogy** for a **euglena**? Explain why or why not.

_____

_____

_____

2. What do a **hammada**, a **veldt**, and a **steppe** have in common?

_____

_____

_____

3. In which country would you be likely to find **dolmades** at an **agora**?

_____

_____

4. What are some similarities and some differences between a **coati** and an **agouti**?

_____

_____

5. Would you rather babysit a child who was **obstreperous** or one who was **amiable**? Why?

_____

_____

6. When might you give an **octogenarian** a **cymbidium**? Explain your answer.

_____

_____

7. If you were a **tyro**, would you attempt to play a piano duet with a **virtuoso**? Why or why not?

_____

_____

Name: _____   **Date:** _____

Building Vocabulary Skills and Strategies, Level 7 • Saddleback Publishing, Inc. ©2004 • 3 Watson, Irvine, CA 92618 • Phone (888) SDL-BACK • www.sdlback.com   15

PRONUNCIATION: VOWEL SOUNDS 1

If you want to impress people, remember this: Correct pronunciation counts!

Directions: Did you know that each vowel can stand for several different sounds? Which words have the same vowel sound as the **boldface** example word in parentheses? Circle two words in each group.

A SOUNDS

1. **short A (hat)**
   back   make
   began   space

2. **long A (day)**
   basic   volcano
   talk   audience

3. **AL (fall)**
   aim   jail
   almost falter

4. **AR (dare)**
   beware straw
   square start

5. **AR (jar)**
   careful hard
   party   parent

6. **schwa A (alone)**
   scald   laid
   another agree

E SOUNDS

1. **short E (end)**
   empty   being
   spell   legal

2. **long E (she)**
   secret elf
   female men

3. **silent e (place)**
   ever   something
   operate safety

4. **ER (her)**
   reflect baker
   camera brief

5. **schwa E (the)**
   happen item
   weapon fine

I SOUNDS

1. **short I (miss)**
   insect dinosaur
   idle   which

2. **long I (rice)**
   jingle wire
   whir   describe

3. **IR (stir)**
   dirty   shirt
   time   rinse

O SOUNDS

1. **short O (not)**
   opera   zero
   problem odor

2. **long O (ago)**
   got   ocean
   cargo   job

3. **OU / OW (out, cow)**
   young   sound
   crow   eyebrow

4. **OI / OY (spoil, boy)**
   voice   period
   joyous youth

5. **broad O (cross)**
   song   tooth
   wood   office

6. **short OO (book)**
   mood   cookie
   wooden zoo

7. **long OO (too)**
   stood   troop
   foot   bamboo

8. **schwa O (riot)**
   joint   canyon
   doily   method

Name: _____   Date: _____

PRONUNCIATION: VOWEL SOUNDS 2

A. Directions: Which words have the same vowel sound as the **boldface** example word in parentheses? Circle two words in each group.

U SOUNDS

1. short U **(sun)**   funny   museum   Utah   summer

2. long U **(use)**   January   jump   human   umpire

3. 1-dot U̇ **(full)**   tuna   bullfrog   murmur   cushion

4. 2-dot Ü **(flute)**   fur   prune   cruel   bully

5. UR **(curl)**   crude   nutrition   turtle   surface

B. Directions: Circle the word that correctly completes each sentence. Check the dictionary if you're not sure.

1. The word *stare* rhymes with (*there* / *here*).

2. The word *high* rhymes with (*aweigh* / *pie*).

3. The word *blown* rhymes with (*flown* / *crown*).

4. The word *measure* rhymes with (*reassure* / *treasure*).

5. They word *greed* rhymes with (*plead* / *dread*).

6. The word *billow* rhymes with (*allow* / *pillow*).

7. The word *about* rhymes with (*fraught* / *sauerkraut*).

8. The word *stood* rhymes with (*hood* / *mood*).

9. The word *aloud* rhymes with (*stowed* / *plowed*).

10. The word *tough* rhymes with (*enough* / *although*).

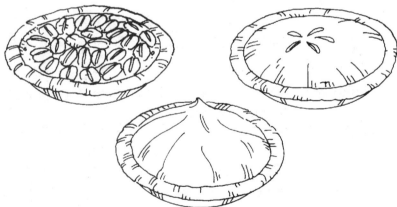

PRONUNCIATION: SILENT LETTERS 1

Remember that many English words have silent letters. If you're not sure how to pronounce a word, look it up!

A. **Directions:** Say each word aloud. Use a dictionary if necessary. Then cross out two words in each group that do *not* have silent letters. Finally, write the silent letter you see in the other two words. The first one has been done for you.

SILENT
LETTER

1. __c__   ~~inspect~~   scenic   ~~color~~   ascend

2. _____   scheduling   showing   happy   honest

3. _____   blow   wander   wilt   wrap

4. _____   water   fetch   often   patted

5. _____   could   flap   talk   tassel

6. _____   gather   align   sugar   gnu

7. _____   buzz   numb   amber   thumb

8. _____   knot   broken   knitting   mark

9. _____   psychology   perhaps   pseudonym   important

B. **Directions:** Think of a word with a silent letter that answers each question.
Write it on the line.

1. What dark color has a silent consonant? _____

2. Name a major organ in your body that has a silent letter. _____

3. Name a school subject that has a silent letter. _____

4. What numbers between one and ten have a silent letter
   or letters? _____

5. What's another word for *climb down*, *sink*, or *slip*? _____

Name: _____   **Date:** _____

18 *Building Vocabulary Skills and Strategies, Level 7* • Saddleback Publishing, Inc. ©2004 • 3 Watson, Irvine, CA 92618 • Phone (888) SDL-BACK • www.sdlback.com

VERBS: GETTING MEANING FROM CONTEXT CLUES

This exercise tests your *verbal* skills. Remember that a *verb* is a word that expresses an <u>action</u> (He *jumped*.) or a <u>state of being</u> (She *is* a good student.).

Directions: Read the incomplete sentences. Then use the **boldface** words as clues to help you figure out the scrambled words.

1. I can **handle** the hand lawn mower, but I don't know how to **(RETEPAO)** _____ the electric one.

2. The wish to succeed that **compels** you to study hard **(ROFECS)** _____ me to keep up with you.

3. If you **grumble** and **(MACINLOP)** _____ about the homework, you'll annoy the teacher.

4. We **compared** and **(TACDROTENS)** _____ the two houses before deciding which one to buy.

5. After Caesar's army **beat** one country, they soon **(QUEDCORNE)** _____ another.

6. Not only did Brendon **hurt** his arm, he also **(JIRNUDE)** _____ his knee.

7. Melissa's ability to **sing and dance** helped her **(REFPORM)** _____ well on stage.

8. First she felt **weak and dizzy**, and then she **(NATFIDE)** _____ .

9. Don't let unworthy goals **attract** you and **(MTTEP)** _____ you to do foolish things.

10. You will **ruin** that shirt if you **(ROCSHC)** _____ it with a hot iron.

Name: _____ **Date:** _____

ADJECTIVES: GETTING MEANING FROM CONTEXT CLUES

Adjectives describe nouns or pronouns by answering such questions as <u>how many</u>? (ten years) or <u>what kind</u>? (leather jacket). Adjectives can make your communication colorful and interesting.

Directions: Read the incomplete sentences. Then use the **boldface** words as clues to help you figure out the scrambled word. Write it on the line.

1. We love our mountain cabin because it is so **calm** and **(CEFPUELA)** _____ there.

2. When the **poor** man was robbed, he became **(TEUDITSTE)** _____.

3. Hiding in the dark, my friends were so quiet their sudden shout of "Surprise!" left me **(CESSHEPELS)** _____.

4. **Shy** Melissa was so **(SHUBFAL)** _____ that she couldn't speak in front of the class.

5. Yesterday was especially **busy**, or **(THECIC)** _____, because Uncle Dan came to visit and the cat had kittens on the couch.

6. The **tough** meat was very **(FIDCUFLIT)** _____ to chew.

7. The **hard** mattress was too **(MIRF)** _____ to be really comfortable.

8. I feel sure of an **easy** A on that **(MILSEP)** _____ math test.

9. The **(HELMUB)** _____ home was decorated in a **plain** style.

10. Our **stroll** in the park filled up our **(SILUELREY)** _____ afternoon.

Name: _____   Date: _____

ADVERBS: GETTING MEANING FROM CONTEXT CLUES

Adverbs answer such questions as <u>when</u>? (arrived *later*), <u>how</u>? (spoke *timidly*), <u>where</u>? (put it *there*), <u>how often</u>? (danced *daily*), and <u>to what extent</u>? (*completely* satisfied).

Directions: Complete each sentence with the most appropriate adverb. Use the **boldface** words as clues. Check a dictionary if you need help with word meaning.

1. It's just a **guess**, but I think there are _____ 15 minutes left on the parking meter. (exactly / approximately / never)

2. After his mother told him to share, the **selfish** little boy _____ offered his playmate one of his toys. (generously / happily / reluctantly)

3. Wanting a **clean** and allergy-proof room, Theresa _____ vacuumed the carpets. (thoroughly / barely / hastily)

4. The **warm**, friendly host _____ welcomed his guests. (shyly / cordially / fearfully)

5. The teacher _____ known as Miss Cooper is **now** called Mrs. Washington. (actually / sadly / formerly)

6. **Basically** and _____, Christopher believes in the value of charity. (fundamentally / shakily / shallowly)

7. Right now I can repay you only _____, but I'll get the **rest** to you soon. (totally / immediately / partially)

8. The hurricane tore _____ through the town, **destroying** all the homes in its path. (peacefully / violently / quietly)

9. "I will _____ sign that confession," said the prisoner, "because I am **innocent**!" (gladly / soon / never)

10. The **perpetual** flame has been burning _____ since John F. Kennedy was buried here. (continuously / intermittently / weakly)

Name: _____ Date: _____

FORMS OF A WORD: ADJECTIVE TO NOUN 1

Adjectives (words that describe) can usually be rewritten as nouns (beautiful → beauty). Remember to keep a dictionary handy to check your spelling.

A. Directions: Notice that all clues are *adjectives*. Complete the crossword puzzle with the *noun* form of each adjective.

ACROSS
4. creative
5. brutal
6. glandular
7. solitary

DOWN
1. accurate
2. hostile
3. prestigious
4. changeable

B. Directions: Now use one of the puzzle answer words to complete each sentence below.

1. Because her thyroid _____ doesn't work properly, Ana's metabolism has slowed down.

2. Have you noticed the recent _____ in that child's behavior?

3. Hector is so proud of his _____ that he's entering it in the art contest.

4. Jeremy needs at least one hour of _____ each day for meditation.

5. Myra's good job gives her _____ in the community.

6. I reported the unkind pet owner's _____ to the police.

7. The mistreated animal exhibited _____ toward his owner.

8. When you measure ingredients for baking, _____ is very important.

Name: _____ **Date:** _____

FORMS OF A WORD: ADJECTIVE TO NOUN 2

Directions: Read the phrases. Then write the *noun* form of each **boldface** adjective. Finally, write an original sentence using that noun.

1. **affectionate** gesture _____

_____

_____

_____

_____

2. **considerate** behavior _____

_____

3. **eternal** love _____

_____

4. **fearless** warrior _____

_____

5. **venomous** poison _____

_____

6. **turbulent** winds _____

_____

7. **suspicious** activity _____

_____

8. **sentimental** journey _____

_____

9. **residential** neighborhood _____

_____

10. **punctual** arrival _____

_____

11. **monotonous** speech _____

_____

Name: _____   **Date:** _____

Building Vocabulary Skills and Strategies, Level 7 • Saddleback Publishing, Inc. ©2004 • 3 Watson, Irvine, CA 92618 • Phone (888) SDL-BACK • www.sdlback.com   29

FORMS OF A WORD: VERB TO ADJECTIVE 1

It isn't difficult to rewrite verbs as adjectives (*enjoy* → *enjoyable*). Remember to keep a dictionary nearby to check your spelling.

A. Directions: Notice that all clue words can be used as *verbs*. Complete the crossword puzzle with the *adjective* form of each verb.

ACROSS
2. prefer
4. filter
6. punctuate
8. dry

DOWN
1. warrant
3. dimple
5. die
7. tie

B. Directions: Write an answer word from the puzzle next to the definition it matches.

1. _____ : no longer living
2. _____ : more desirable
3. _____ : having a small hollow on the cheek or chin
4. _____ : describing water or other fluid that has had its impurities removed
5. _____ : describing something that has had all the water removed
6. _____ : said or done with special force

C. Directions: Write sentences using the adjective form of each verb listed.

1. *believe* _____
2. *enjoy* _____
3. *prefer* _____

Name: _____   Date: _____

FORMS OF A WORD: VERB TO ADJECTIVE 2

Directions: First write the *adjective* form of each **boldface** word. Then write an original sentence using that adjective.

1. to **sustain** a note _____

_____

_____

_____

_____

2. to **warp** a piece of wood _____

_____

3. to **reject** a plan _____

_____

4. to **radiate** light _____

_____

5. to **rebel** against an oppressor _____

_____

6. to **recognize** a friend _____

_____

7. to **excel** in a sport _____

_____

8. to **succeed** in a job _____

_____

9. to **modify** a recipe _____

_____

10. to **persist** in a task _____

_____

11. to **intend** to get organized _____

_____

Name: _____ **Date:** _____

Building Vocabulary Skills and Strategies, Level 7 • Saddleback Publishing, Inc. ©2004 • 3 Watson, Irvine, CA 92618 • Phone (888) SDL-BACK • www.sdlback.com 31

FORMS OF A WORD: NOUN TO VERB 1

How do you rewrite a noun as a verb? Example: *competition → compete*. Some of these changes can be tricky, so keep a dictionary handy.

A. Directions: Notice that the **boldface** clues are *nouns* (naming words). Puzzle answers are the *verb* form of each noun. Check a dictionary if you need help.

ACROSS
3. a careful **consumer**
4. window **draperies**
5. a lucky **rescue**
6. a feeling of **hatred**

DOWN
1. an exciting **drama**
2. a young **dependent**
3. a difficult **complication**

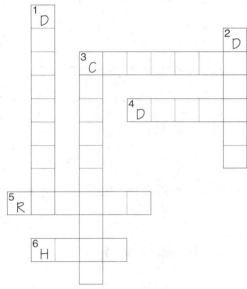

B. Directions: Now use one of the puzzle answer words to complete each sentence below.

1. The lifeguard will _____ the desperate swimmer.

2. I absolutely _____ the smell of skunks.

3. Our large family can _____ two loaves of bread a day.

4. Sheryl and Joe seem to _____ every unimportant little event.

5. Those lazy teenagers _____ on their parents for everything.

6. This new requirement will _____ our task considerably.

7. We can _____ the fabric gracefully around the display.

Name: _____   Date: _____

FORMS OF A WORD: NOUN TO VERB 2

Directions: First write the *verb* form of each **boldface** noun. Then write an original sentence using that verb.

1. another **postponement** _____

_____

2. engine **lubrication** _____

_____

3. **conviction** of the suspect _____

_____

4. an uncomfortable **confrontation** _____

_____

5. regular **correspondence** _____

_____

6. a surprising **development** _____

_____

7. military **organization** _____

_____

8. shallow **penetration** _____

_____

9. total **paralysis** _____

_____

10. an interesting **narrative** _____

_____

11. accurate **representation** _____

_____

Name: _____   **Date:** _____

Building Vocabulary Skills and Strategies, Level 7 • Saddleback Publishing, Inc. ©2004 • 3 Watson, Irvine, CA 92618 • Phone (888) SDL-BACK • www.sdlback.com   33

JUST FOR FUN: WORD LADDERS 1

Word play makes vocabulary-building a lot more fun!
Now have a good time discovering how much
difference a letter or two can make!

A. Directions: Change one letter in each **boldface** word to complete the word ladder.
Use the clues to help you figure out the words. As an example, the first
one has been done for you.

1. **RAKE**

   bake   do to bread

   lake   body of water

   cake   birthday treat

2. **CARE**

   _____ without clothing

   _____ a bold move

   _____ big bunny

3. **TIDE**

   _____ travel by car

   _____ a square has four

   _____ opposite of seek

4. **ZEST**

   _____ a bother

   _____ exam

   _____ good, better

5. **WEAK**

   _____ a bird has one

   _____ drip from a faucet

   _____ type of wood

6. **TOOT**

   _____ type of shoe

   _____ a plant has one

   _____ pirate treasure

B. Directions: Now change *two* letters in each word to complete the following word ladders.

1. **QUACK**

   _____ for a train

   _____ a pile

   _____ a dark color

2. **SHEEP**

   _____ another word for *crawl*

   _____ take a nap

   _____ a baby bird's sound

3. **SPILL**

   _____ to make cold

   _____ motionless

   _____ to barbecue

4. **STAKE**

   _____ to stop a car

   _____ a piece of snow

   _____ a male duck

Name: _____   **Date:** _____

34   *Building Vocabulary Skills and Strategies, Level 7* • Saddleback Publishing, Inc. ©2004 • 3 Watson, Irvine, CA 92618 • Phone (888) SDL-BACK • www.sdlback.com

JUST FOR FUN: WORD LADDERS 2

A. Directions: Make new words by adding one letter at the *beginning* of each short word. The first one has been done for you.

1. _s_ talk
   _s_ pin
   _s_ age

2. ___lash
   ___lag
   ___act

3. ___rain
   ___lob
   ___old

4. ___ale
   ___ant
   ___arch

5. ___art
   ___ore
   ___reek

6. ___one
   ___ail
   ___either

B. Directions: This time you will make new words by adding one letter at the *end* of each short word.

1. plan___
   for___
   car___

2. pan___
   tan___
   ban___

3. for___
   nor___
   war___

4. tar___
   see___
   dam___

C. Directions: Now add a letter somewhere *inside* the short word to make a new word. The first one has been done for you.

1. cap _clap, camp, chap, or carp_
2. fame _____
3. base _____
4. bag _____
5. cot _____
6. hug _____
7. pose _____
8. lie _____

Name: _____   Date: _____

Building Vocabulary Skills and Strategies, Level 7 • Saddleback Publishing, Inc. ©2004 • 3 Watson, Irvine, CA 92618 • Phone (888) SDL-BACK • www.sdlback.com   35

MAKING COMPOUND WORDS 1

Some words are made up of two smaller words. Sunflower and airline are examples of familiar compound words.

A. Directions:

Combine words from the first list with words from the second list to make compound words. Write a letter to show which words go together. The first one has been done for you.

1. _j_ hair *cut*   a. crow

2. ____ wrist_____   b. back

3. ____ air_____   c. watch

4. ____ out_____   d. fall

5. ____ scare_____   e. port

6. ____ touch_____   f. ware

7. ____ water_____   g. bite

8. ____ over_____   h. cake

9. ____ pan_____   i. side

10. ____ sky_____   j. cut

11. ____ silver_____   k. fast

12. ____ paper_____   l. down

13. ____ break_____   m. scraper

B. Directions:

In the squares below, draw pictures to illustrate three of the compound words you made. Write the word under each picture.

WORD: _____

WORD: _____

WORD: _____

Name: _____

Date: _____

36   *Building Vocabulary Skills and Strategies, Level 7* • Saddleback Publishing, Inc. ©2004 • 3 Watson, Irvine, CA 92618 • Phone (888) SDL-BACK • www.sdlback.com

MAKING COMPOUND WORDS 2

A. Directions: Use vowels (a, e, i, o, u) to complete the compound words.

1. A ballerina sometimes dances on her t_pt___s.

2. Mom said to put the clean dishes in the c_pb___rd.

3. Did you ever make tea from p_pp_rm_nt leaves?

4. The sp_tl_ght was on the star of the play as she sang her solo.

5. The baby sits in the h_ghch___r to eat her meals.

6. Lester likes to wear a sw___tsh_rt featuring his school's logo.

7. There's a w_ndm_ll in the park's tulip garden.

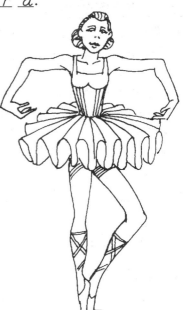

B. Directions: Solve the crossword puzzle with familiar compound words. Use the clues for help.

ACROSS
1. a mental image of a scene from the past
4. combination of clothes that go together
6. a long braid of hair
7. use this to wash dishes

DOWN
2. person in charge at the beach
3. one way to get to school
5. a pet in a bowl of water
6. mail sent from your vacation

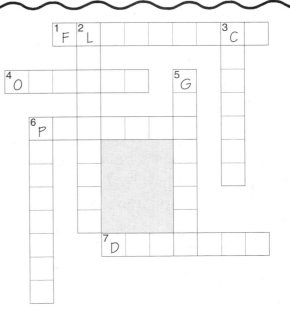

Name: _____ Date: _____

COMPOUND WORDS: *HEAD* AND *FOOT* 1

Heads up! It's time to show what you know about compound words.

A. **Directions:** First write *head* or *foot* to complete each compound word. Then draw a line to match each word with its meaning.

1. _____phone   a. mark left in wet sand

2. _____bridge   b. big print in a newspaper

3. _____note   c. piece of furniture that goes with a chair

4. _____lights   d. device for listening to music privately

5. _____print   e. construction that goes over a river

6. _____stool   f. information at the bottom of a page

7. _____line   g. lamps in the front of a car (or lights on a stage)

B. **Directions:** Use words from the box to complete the answer words.
Then solve the crossword puzzle.

ache	ball	band	board	hunter	locker	quarters

ACROSS

2. The corporate *head* _____ found a good employee for the position.

5. *Foot* _____ can be a very violent sport.

6. Carol uses a *head* _____ to keep the hair out of her eyes.

DOWN

1. Marge has a painful *head* _____.

3. His company's *head* _____ is located in Chicago.

4. The *foot* _____ of the bed is handcarved.

5. The soldier's *foot* _____ was kept very neat.

Name: _____   Date: _____

38 *Building Vocabulary Skills and Strategies, Level 7* • Saddleback Publishing, Inc. ©2004 • 3 Watson, Irvine, CA 92618 • Phone (888) SDL-BACK • www.sdlback.com

COMPOUND WORDS: *HEAD* AND *FOOT* 2

Directions: Use the context clues to help you figure out the incomplete compound words. Check a dictionary if you need help.

1. Some Native Americans used to wear beautiful *head*_____ made of feathers.

2. A mountain climber must get a good *foot*_____ as he climbs.

3. The fancy *head*_____ of that bed is made of solid maple.

4. Burt came hurtling down the waterslide *head*_____.

5. The *foot*_____ carried by her shop includes shoes, boots, and sandals.

6. The telephone operator wore a *head*_____ to keep her hands free.

7. Wanda could hear heavy *foot*_____ coming up the stairs.

8. Kim likes to think of herself as "*foot*_____ and fancy free."

9. We made good *head*_____ in spite of the strong wind.

10. The senior citizens enjoyed walking on the *foot*_____ by the river.

11. Sixteen runners competed in the *foot*_____ through the woods.

12. The wrestler held his opponent in a mighty *head*_____.

Name: _____   **Date:** _____

Building Vocabulary Skills and Strategies, Level 7 • Saddleback Publishing, Inc. ©2004 • 3 Watson, Irvine, CA 92618 • Phone (888) SDL-BACK • www.sdlback.com   39

COMPOUND WORDS: *AIR* AND *WATER* 1

A. Directions: Unscramble the words to complete the sentences. Hint: All the scrambled words begin with *air* or *water*.

1. Doris stores beans and rice in **(TIHATRIG)** _____ containers.

2. The tiny dragonfly stopped to rest on the **(TYLWILEAR)** _____.

3. An **(IRALIMA)** _____ letter takes two days to get here from Dallas.

4. A leak caused the boat to become **(GETDARLOWEG)** _____.

5. We got to the **(ROITARP)** _____ early to go through security.

6. Tom led us on a hike to see a spectacular **(TELWALFAR)** _____.

B. Directions: Use words from the box to complete the answer words. Then use the completed words to solve the puzzle.

brush	colors	front	line	melon	sick	waves

ACROSS

2. Radio signals travel over the
   air _____.

4. Which do you like better,
   water _____ or oil paintings?

5. Whenever she flies, Amy gets
   air _____.

6. We ate a big *water* _____
   and kept the seeds for planting.

7. The *water* _____ on the
   ship is higher when the hold
   is heavy with cargo.

DOWN

1. The seafood restaurant is located
   on the *water* _____.

3. We used an *air* _____ to
   apply paint to the fence.

Name: _____   Date: _____

40 *Building Vocabulary Skills and Strategies, Level 7* • Saddleback Publishing, Inc. ©2004 • 3 Watson, Irvine, CA 92618 • Phone (888) SDL-BACK • www.sdlback.com

COMPOUND WORDS: *AIR* AND *WATER* 2

Directions: Use context clues to help you figure out the compound words beginning with *air* and *water*. Check a dictionary if you need more ideas.

1. Ducks, geese, and swans are different kinds of *water*_____.

2. Good-quality paper often has a *water*_____, a design produced by pressure during manufacture.

3. Tests proved that the helicopter was *air*_____, or safe for flying.

4. This vinyl raincoat is guaranteed to be *water*_____.

5. The fighter jets began an *air*_____ on the city.

6. The cook added *water*_____, an edible plant related to the nasturtium, to our sandwiches.

7. That hang glider has been *air*_____ for 30 minutes.

8. This will be little Alice's first flight in an *air*_____.

9. The flashlight was encased in a *water*_____ container.

10. That country does not allow military jets to fly in its *air*_____.

11. Niagara Falls is a very large and famous *water*_____.

Name: _____   **Date:** _____

Building Vocabulary Skills and Strategies, Level 7 • Saddleback Publishing, Inc. ©2004 • 3 Watson, Irvine, CA 92618 • Phone (888) SDL-BACK • www.sdlback.com   41

COMPOUND WORDS: *SUN* AND *WIND* 1

A. Directions: First write *sun* or *wind* to complete each compound word. Then draw a line to match each word with its meaning.

1. _____bag

2. _____glasses

3. _____sock

4. _____down

5. _____rise

6. _____breaker

7. _____dial

a. another word for sunset

b. another word for dawn

c. a lightweight jacket

d. a person who talks too much

e. a device that indicates time with shadows

f. fashion item that protects eyes

g. a cloth tube attached to the top of a pole that shows which way the wind is blowing

B. Directions: Use words from the box to complete the puzzle answers.

burn	storms	surfed	shield	tan	roof	bonnet	fall

ACROSS

1. *Wind* _____ can uproot even very big trees.

4. *Sun* _____ can inflame your skin and cause blisters.

6. Barry *wind* _____ on the bay.

7. Lydia got a great *sun* _____ in Hawaii.

8. We need new *wind* _____ wipers on our car.

DOWN

2. While gardening, Elizabeth wore a pink *sun* _____.

3. Sam's new car has a *sun* _____.

5. Tim's surprise inheritance was quite a *wind* _____.

Name: _____

Date: _____

42 *Building Vocabulary Skills and Strategies, Level 7* • Saddleback Publishing, Inc. ©2004 • 3 Watson, Irvine, CA 92618 • Phone (888) SDL-BACK • www.sdlback.com

COMPOUND WORDS: SUN AND WIND 2

Directions: Use context clues to help you figure out the compound words. If you need help completing the words, check a dictionary.

1. A wind_____ is a large sailing ship that is especially fast.

2. A beautiful sun_____ found its way through the thick trees and shone on the forest floor.

3. The wind_____ factor made the frigid air seem even colder.

4. Holland is famous for its great number of wind_____.

5. By sitting under a sun_____, you can get an even tan without going outside.

6. Henry choked when he got a piece of chicken caught in his wind_____.

7. Betty likes to sun_____ by lying in a hammock in her backyard.

8. Bluegill and black bass are types of sun_____ , which swim in freshwater lakes and rivers.

9. Ellen likes the wind_____, casual look for her hair.

10. Annie puts sun_____ on her baby before taking him outdoors in the sun.

11. A sun_____ is a tall annual plant with big yellow blooms.

CHOOSING PRECISE WORDS 1

Choosing words with exact meanings greatly improves your communication skills!

A. Directions: Write **G** for *general* or **S** for *specific* to identify each word below. Then write a specific example for each general word or a word that names a general category for each specific word. The first two have been done for you.

1. _G_ dessert _ice cream_
2. _S_ autumn _season_
3. ___ animal _____
4. ___ diamond _____
5. ___ jewelry _____
6. ___ flower _____
7. ___ green _____
8. ___ salmon _____

B. Directions: Make 10 pairs of synonyms from the words in the box. Check a dictionary if you're not sure of word meanings. Then write the words under the proper headings. The first one has been done for you.

abhor	adore	apologize	admire	alone
absurd	atone	dislike	disagree	domination
entertain	ecstatic	enthrall	foolish	isolated
hobby	glad	obsession	influence	oppose

	MORE INTENSE	LESS INTENSE		MORE INTENSE	LESS INTENSE
1.	abhor	dislike	6.		
2.			7.		
3.			8.		
4.			9.		
5.			10.		

Name: _____ Date: _____

CHOOSING PRECISE WORDS 2

Have you heard? A *thesaurus* is the best place to "shop for synonyms."

Directions: First, unscramble the first specific synonym for each **boldface** general word. Then write original sentences using any two of the specific words. The first one has been done for you as an example.

GENERAL WORD	MORE SPECIFIC WORDS

1. **change**   **(RAVY)** _vary_, modify, evolve, grow, ripen, mellow, mature, transform

    a. *If the peaches are too hard, wait until they ripen.*
    b. *If your plans don't work out, modify them.*

2. **entertain**   **(SEAMU)** _____, cheer, please, delight, divert, charm, captivate, stimulate

    a. _____
    b. _____

3. **interesting**   **(GANEGGNI)** _____, pleasing, enchanting, satisfying, fascinating, absorbing

    a. _____
    b. _____

4. **answer**   **(SENDROP)** _____, echo, react, rebut, argue, retort, remark

    a. _____
    b. _____

5. **run**   **(SNIRPT)** _____, amble, gallop, canter, scamper, race, rush, dash

    a. _____
    b. _____

6. **sad**   **(MUGL)** _____, sorrowful, downcast, gloomy, depressed, morose, grieved

    a. _____
    b. _____

Name: _____   **Date:** _____

GREEK ROOTS 1

If you know Greek roots, you can unlock the meaning of many English words.

ROOT	MEANING	EXAMPLE	ROOT	MEANING	EXAMPLE
cycl	circle, ring	bicycle, cyclone	dem	people	democracy, demogogue
gram	letter, written	telegram, diagram	gnos	know	agnostic, diagnostic
phon	sound	phonograph, telephone	lith	stone	lithograph, monolith
cardi	heart	cardiac, cardiogram	andr	man	androgynous, androphobia

Directions: Use the roots in the box above to complete the words in the sentences.

1. According to the doctor, Beth's p r o _ _ _ _ i s was good.

2. The t e l e _ _ _ _ with the shocking news arrived at midnight.

3. My mother's _ _ _ _ o l o g i s t is a highly respected heart doctor.

4. The toddler enjoyed her new red t r i _ _ _ _ e.

5. We enjoyed the s y m _ _ _ _ y at the new center for the arts.

6. This tool dates from the p a l e o _ _ _ _ i c age.

7. The AIDS e p i _ _ _ i c is especially devastating in Africa.

8. A woman who has two or more husbands at the same time is guilty of p o l y _ _ _ _ y.

9. A m i c r o _ _ _ _ e can help a speaker's voice carry to the back of the room.

10. The study of _ _ _ _ _ i c s helps children relate letters to their sounds.

11. The _ _ _ _ _ o p s has one large round eye in the center of his forehead.

12. Dad is a Republican, but Mom is a _ _ _ _ o c r a t.

Name: _____ Date: _____

46 Building Vocabulary Skills and Strategies, Level 7 • Saddleback Publishing, Inc. ©2004 • 3 Watson, Irvine, CA 92618 • Phone (888) SDL-BACK • www.sdlback.com

GREEK ROOTS 2

You can often guess the meaning of a Greek root by thinking about the words in which it appears. For example: *archenemy*, *monarch*. Why, the root *arch* must mean "chief"!

A. Directions: Notice the root in both example words. Then draw a line to connect each root with its meaning. Check a dictionary if you need help.

1. *dog*matic, *dog*matism   a. shape
2. *pod*iatrist, tri*pod*   b. love
3. *paleo*ntology, *paleo*lithic   c. foot
4. *neo*classic, *neo*phyte   d. opinion
5. meta*morph*osis, *morph*ology   e. old
6. *phil*osophy, *phil*anthropist   f. new

B. Directions: Use the example words to help you guess the meaning of the root.

1. *opt*ician, *opt*ometrist   The root *opt* must mean _____.

2. claustro*phobia*, aqua*phobia*   The root *phobia* must mean _____.

3. *the*ology, a*the*ist   The root *the* must mean _____.

C. Directions: Read the root, its meaning, and the example word. Then add one more word that includes this root.

ROOT	MEANING	EXAMPLES	
1. *kine, cine*	movement	*kinetic* , _____
2. *lys*	break down	*analysis* , _____
3. *mania*	madness	*pyromania* , _____
4. *esth*	feeling	*esthetic* , _____

Name: _____   Date: _____

LATIN ROOTS 1

Many English words contain Latin roots. The Latin roots in the chart will certainly help to complete this exercise!

ROOT	MEANING	EXAMPLE	ROOT	MEANING	EXAMPLE
don	give	*donation*	cline	lean	*incline*
cur	care	*manicure*	cogn	know	*incognito*
cord	heart	*cordial*	man	hand	*manual*
mar	sea	*maritime*	ped	foot	*pedal*

Directions: Use the roots in the box to complete the words in the sentences.

1. The s u b _ _ _ _ _ _ _ was underwater for a week-long training exercise.

2. Darlene had changed so much that Darryl hardly r e _ _ _ _ _ i z e d her.

3. The _ _ _ u s c r i p t for the new book was more than one thousand pages.

4. Theresa gave her guests a very _ _ _ _ i a l welcome.

5. Bob likes to relax in his red r e _ _ _ _ _ r when he gets home from work.

6. The crosswalk was designed for the safety of _ _ _ e s t r i a n s.

7. The young couple _ _ _ a t e d a bag of clothing to the charity.

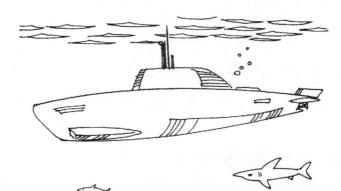

8. The doctor told Thomas that his disease was easily _ _ _ a b l e.

9. When Paul graduates from high school, he wants to join the _ _ _ i n e s.

10. Shannon's grandfather owned a large _ _ _ u f a c t u r i n g plant.

11. Unlike whales, most mammals are q u a d r u _ _ _ s.

LATIN ROOTS 2

> Think about the words in which a root appears. Examples: *luminous, illuminate, luminescent*. The root *lum* must mean "light"!

A. Directions: Circle the word that makes sense in each sentence.

1. *automobile, mobile, mobility*
   The root *mob* must mean
   (self / **move** / money).

2. *spectacle, spectator, inspect*
   The root *spec* must mean
   (**see** / glasses / sport).

3. *migrate, immigration, migratory*
   The root *migr* must mean (birds / people / **move**).

4. *fidelity, confidence, infidel*
   The root *fid* must mean (**faith** / sound / warrior).

5. *bellicose, belligerent, rebellion*
   The root *belli* must mean (calm / **war** / justice).

6. *community, communal, communism*
   The root *commun* must mean (political / inexpensive / **common**).

B. Directions: Read the meaning of the root and the example words. Then add one more word that contains this root.

ROOT	MEANING	EXAMPLES
1. alt	high	*altitude*, *alto*, _____
2. grat	pleasing	*gratify*, *congratulate*, _____
3. doc	teach	*doctrine*, *doctor*, _____
4. pater	father	*paternal*, *patriarch*, _____

Name: _____ Date: _____

PREFIXES 1

A *prefix* is a group of letters added to the beginning of a word to change its meaning.

PREFIX	MEANING	EXAMPLE	PREFIX	MEANING	EXAMPLE
prot	first	*protagonist*	**poly**	many	*polysyllabic*
quint	five	*quintet*	**bene**	good	*benefit*
oct	eight	*octagon*	**com**	with	*combine*
extra	beyond	*extracurricular*	**contra**	against	*contradict*

Directions: Review the material in the chart above. Then use the prefixes to complete the words in the sentences. Use context clues for help.

1. Chris designed the _ _ _ _ _ o t y p e for that new automobile model.

2. Some religions encourage _ _ _ _ g a m y, the practice of having many wives.

3. Diane is one of the famous _ _ _ _ _ _ u p l e t s born in our city 15 years ago.

4. This particular medicine is _ _ _ _ _ _ _ _ i n d i c a t e d for your condition.

5. Our very generous _ _ _ _ _ f a c t o r prefers to remain anonymous.

6. Your friendship is a great joy and _ _ _ f o r t to me.

7. That talented girl has an _ _ _ _ _ _ o r d i n a r y singing voice.

8. Over the years, our jazz band has grown from a trio to an _ _ _ e t.

9. A _ _ _ _ n o m i a l is a math expression consisting of more than two terms.

10. The last church service of the day was a beautiful _ _ _ _ d i c t i o n.

Name: _____ **Date:** _____

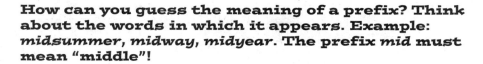

PREFIXES 2

How can you guess the meaning of a prefix? Think about the words in which it appears. Example: *midsummer, midway, midyear*. The prefix *mid* must mean "middle"!

A. Directions: Circle the word that correctly completes each sentence.

1. *automatic, autobiography*

    The prefix *auto* must mean
    (other / quick / **self**).

2. *imbalance, immature*

    The prefix *im* must mean
    (young / **not** / steady).

3. *pseudonym, pseudoclassic*

    The prefix *pseudo* must mean
    (**false** / true / old).

4. *megabyte, megaton*

    The prefix *mega* must mean
    (small / **million** / loud).

5. *circumference, circulate*

    The prefix *circu* must mean
    (area / air / **around**).

6. *microfilm, microscope*

    The prefix *micro* must mean
    (**small** / large / see).

B. Directions: The prefixes *en-* and *em-* both mean "in." Complete each word below with the correct prefix.

1. The two sisters __*embraced*__ when they met at the family reunion.

2. Inez will __*enclose*__ a self-addressed, stamped envelope with her request.

3. The desperate bookkeeper decided to __*embezzle*__ money from her employer.

4. Emma likes to __*embroider*__ her initials on her clothing.

5. Stu was __*enchanted*__ by the beauty of his grandmother's old-fashioned garden.

6. Parents need to __*encourage*__ their children to do their best.

Name: _____ **Date:** _____

SUFFIXES 1

A *suffix* is a group of letters added to the end of a word to change its meaning. The suffixes in the box below indicate the "state" or "quality" of something.

SUFFIX	EXAMPLE	SUFFIX	EXAMPLE	SUFFIX	EXAMPLE	SUFFIX	EXAMPLE
ancy	vacancy	hood	falsehood	ization	civilization	ty	loyalty
ery, ry	imagery	ism	heroism	ude	gratitude	or	error

Directions: Use the suffixes to complete the words in the sentences.

1. Luckily, the apartment building had a two-bedroom v a c _ _ _ _ _.

2. Silas faced every misfortune in his life with f o r t i _ _ _ _.

3. Sara and Erin are enjoying a very happy c h i l d _ _ _ _.

4. Over the years, the United States has suffered greatly because of r a c _ _ _.

5. The poet e. e. cummings did not follow the rules of c a p i t a l _ _ _ _ _ _ _.

6. The reward for h o n e s _ _ is knowing that you did the right thing.

7. The p a l l _ _ in the sick child's face was quite alarming.

8. The soldier exhibited extreme b r a v e _ _ during the long battle.

9. The s t a n d a r d _ _ _ _ _ _ _ of shoe sizes makes it easy to buy footwear.

10. Heloise's belief in p a c i f _ _ _ prevents her from supporting any war.

11. The f e r v _ _ of his political ideas sets him apart from most people.

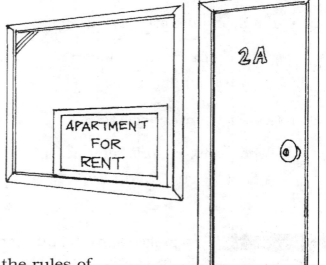

Name: _____ Date: _____

SUFFIXES 2

Many different suffixes have exactly the same meaning. This can be confusing—but I'm sure you're up to the challenge!

A. Directions: Complete each word below with one of the **boldface** suffixes.

The suffixes **-al, -ary, -esque,** *and* **-ular** *all mean "relating to."*

1. her m a t e r n _ _ instincts
2. a tall and s t a t u _ _ _ _ _ model
3. a c i r c _ _ _ _ _ argument
4. full m i l i t _ _ _ honors
5. a p i c t u r _ _ _ _ _ scene
6. a p o p _ _ _ _ candidate
7. his n a t u r _ _ inclinations

B. Directions: Complete each word below with one of the **boldface** suffixes.

The suffixes **-ful, -ose, -ous,** *and* **-ulent** *all mean "full of."*

1. After watching the scary movie, the little boys were f e a r _ _ _ _ of the dark.
2. T u r b _ _ _ _ _ _ waves threatened to sink the small fishing boat.
3. Jeff was feeling n e r v _ _ _ _ before his job interview.
4. The accident victim was c o m a t _ _ _ _ for several days.
5. Rita is s u c c e s s _ _ _ at almost everything she tries.
6. The coronation of the young queen was truly g l o r i _ _ _.

Name: _____ **Date:** _____

NEAR MISSES 1

Some words can be confusing if you're not careful. Watch out for the troublemakers!

Directions: Circle the word that correctly completes each sentence. Look it up if you're not sure!

1. When moving cars have a (collision / collusion), both drivers and passengers can get hurt.

2. Over time, eating too much food will make your waistline (expend / expand).

3. After Myra lost so much weight, all her clothes were too (loose / lose).

4. The Martinez family told us they want to (adapt / adopt) a child.

5. After college, Beverly has decided to (pursue / peruse) a career in journalism.

6. Steven is in charge of the (personnel / personal) department in his company.

7. After running for three hours, Sylvia (finely / finally) crossed the finish line.

8. When it comes to books, Stanley has a (veracious / voracious) appetite.

9. Sue's many friends will continue to (perpetuate / perpetrate) her memory.

10. The lost hiker was hungry; he had been (depraved / deprived) of food for three days.

11. Caroline wrote information about her appointments on her (calendar / colander).

Name: _____   Date: _____

NEAR MISSES 2

A. Directions: Use eight of the *wrong* word choices in the previous exercise to complete the crossword puzzle.

ACROSS

3. fail to win
5. to commit (a crime)
7. to read or study
8. a secret agreement for a wrongful purpose

DOWN

1. a strainer
2. completely wicked
4. truthful
6. in an excellent manner

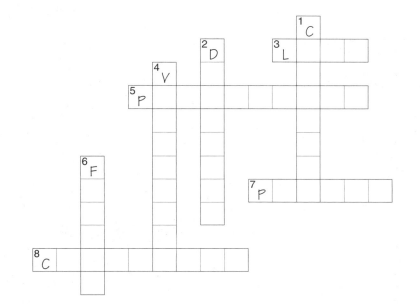

B. Directions: Write a letter to match each **boldface** "near miss" word with its meaning.

1. _____ **quite**   a. to look forward
2. _____ **quiet**   b. by means of
3. _____ **through**   c. relating to mankind
4. _____ **thorough**   d. very
5. _____ **expect**   e. kind
6. _____ **suspect**   f. to order
7. _____ **human**   g. not noisy
8. _____ **humane**   h. to praise
9. _____ **command**   i. complete
10. _____ **commend**   j. to mistrust

SYNONYMS: NOUNS 1

You know that *synonyms* are words with the same or nearly the same meaning. The more synonyms you know, the richer your vocabulary will be!

Directions: First write a letter to match each **boldface** noun with its synonym. Then find another synonym in the box for each pair of words. Write it on the line. Hint: You will *not* use all the words in the box. The first one has been done for you.

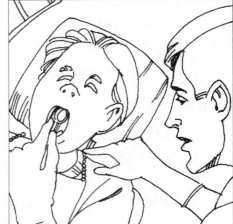

admission	cavity	exaggeration	haste
awning	comedy	flattery	hatred
ban	dwelling	glint	instructor

1. _b_ **affirmation,** ____admission____   a. abode

2. ____ **pit,** _____   b. admittance

3. ____ **home,** _____   c. compliments

4. ____ **praise,** _____   d. elaboration

5. ____ **prohibition,** _____   e. hole

6. ____ **hyperbole,** _____   f. hurry

7. ____ **gleam,** _____   g. loathing

8. ____ **scramble,** _____   h. sparkle

9. ____ **abhorrence,** _____   i. taboo

10. ____ **professor,** _____   j. tutor

Name: _____   **Date:** _____

SYNONYMS: NOUNS 2

Directions: Unscramble the *synonym* of the other **boldface** words in each sentence.

1. You carry a **(CACKURKS)** _____, or **knapsack**, the same way you carry a **backpack**.

2. If you want words meaning the same as **(GAMINICA)** _____, you could use **enchanter** or **necromancer**.

3. The team you're playing against could be called your **opponent**, **foe**, or **(MECIRTOPTO)** _____.

4. Victoria felt not only **excitement** and **emotion** for dancing—she had a real **(SONPIAS)** _____ for it.

5. When the **assault** began, those in the castle had no idea the **onslaught** would be even worse than the last **(GESIE)** _____.

6. The **(SRTOM)** _____ at sea began as a **squall** and quickly turned into a **tempest**.

7. We need a large **receptacle** for these flowers. Please get the blue **(ASEV)** _____ or the yellow **urn**.

8. The **lure** of the ocean was such an **attraction** for Sam that he gave in to the **(PITONETMAT)** _____ to buy a boat.

9. Before the trial, Myra gave a **statement**, or **declaration**. At the trial, she gave sworn **(SITOYMENT)** _____.

Name: _____ **Date:** _____

Building Vocabulary Skills and Strategies, Level 7 • Saddleback Publishing, Inc. ©2004 • 3 Watson, Irvine, CA 92618 • Phone (888) SDL-BACK • www.sdlback.com **57**

SYNONYMS: VERBS 1

In a thesaurus, how many synonyms can find you for the word good?

A. Directions: Add an appropriate word from the box to each list of synonyms.
Hint: You will *not* use all the words in the box.

| admit | assure | catch | expel | induce | insult | invalidate | toss | uplift | waver |

1. _____
   taunt
   ridicule
   jeer

2. _____
   guarantee
   warrant
   pledge

3. _____
   initiate
   inaugurate
   introduce

4. _____
   falter
   fluctuate
   hesitate

5. _____
   cancel
   nullify
   repeal

6. _____
   acknowledge
   concede
   confess

7. _____
   grab
   snare
   capture

8. _____
   heave
   throw
   fling

9. _____
   banish
   exile
   deport

B. Directions: Now find two synonyms in the box for each **boldface** verb. Add the synonyms to each list. Hint: You will *not* use all the words.

appraise	burn	handy	deserve	harass	prefer	untwist
assess	char	curve	differ	justify	suitable	victimize
bend	choose	dawdle	digress	linger	untangle	

1. **merit**
   _____
   _____

2. **opt**
   _____
   _____

3. **persecute**
   _____
   _____

4. **unravel**
   _____
   _____

5. **scald**
   _____
   _____

6. **evaluate**
   _____
   _____

7. **convenient**
   _____
   _____

8. **vary**
   _____
   _____

9. **warp**
   _____
   _____

Name: _____   Date: _____

SYNONYMS: VERBS 2

A. Directions: First read each group of synonyms. Then unscramble the word that heads each list.

1. **EDAL** _____
   direct
   oversee
   supervise

2. **NAXIEME** _____
   observe
   scrutinize
   inspect

3. **VOREC** _____
   hide
   screen
   mask

4. **CHUNP** _____
   hit
   strike
   knock

5. **LOSI** _____
   stain
   dirt
   tarnish

6. **ROSUNURD** _____
   enclose
   encircle
   encompass

B. Directions: Write synonyms of your own for the following verbs.

1. sleep / _____

2. smudge / _____

3. reek / _____

4. lure / _____

5. influence / _____

C. Directions: Now write original sentences using synonyms for these verbs:
cherish, cram, displease, intend, overcome, pose, and *sulk.*

1. _____

2. _____

3. _____

4. _____

5. _____

6. _____

7. _____

Name: _____   **Date:** _____

Building Vocabulary Skills and Strategies, Level 7 • Saddleback Publishing, Inc. ©2004 • 3 Watson, Irvine, CA 92618 • Phone (888) SDL-BACK • www.sdlback.com   59

SYNONYMS: ADJECTIVES 1

Ready for some more *synonym* practice? This time let's work with *adjectives* (describing words).

Directions: First write a letter to match each **boldface** adjective with its synonym. Then find *another* synonym in the box for each pair of words. Write it on the line. Hint: You will *not* use all the words in the box. The first one has been done for you.

aged	ambitious	basic	miniature
changeable	received	flimsy	genuine
hardy	intellectual	irritated	irregular

1. _d_ **authenticated,** _genuine_____   a. irked

2. ____ **elderly,** _____   b. cerebral

3. ____ **aspiring,** _____   c. accepted

4. ____ **bothered,** _____   d. validated

5. ____ **fragile,** _____   e. delicate

6. ____ **variable,** _____   f. diminutive

7. ____ **welcomed,** _____   g. old

8. ____ **tiny,** _____   h. strong

9. ____ **tough,** _____   i. hopeful

10. ____ **mental,** _____   j. differing

Name: _____   **Date:** _____

SYNONYMS: ADJECTIVES 2

A. Directions: Find two synonyms in the box for each **boldface** adjective. Write the synonyms on the lines. Hint: You will *not* use all the words in the box.

astute	dependable	dangerous	fancy	loyal	male
manly	pictorial	risky	scenic	sharp	showy
shriveled	triumphant	unique	unusual	uncontrollable	willful

1. **ornamental** shrubs

   _____

   _____

2. a **masculine** attitude

   _____

   _____

3. a **reliable** friend

   _____

   _____

4. a **treacherous** river

   _____

   _____

5. a **novel** approach

   _____

   _____

6. a **picturesque** location

   _____

   _____

B. Directions: Think of a synonym for each **boldface** adjective below. Write it on the line.

1. a **contagious** disease

   _____

2. a **feminine** trait

   _____

3. **delicious** foods

   _____

4. a **defiant** subject

   _____

5. an **exceptional** bargain

   _____

6. a **microscopic** speck

   _____

Name: _____   **Date:** _____

SYNONYMS: ADVERBS 1

Remember that an *adverb* modifies or qualifies a verb, adjective, or another adverb. An adverb answers such questions as *when? how? where? how often?* and *to what extent?*

A. Directions: Write a letter to match each **boldface** adverb with its synonym.

1. ____ **thankfully**
2. ____ **accurately**
3. ____ **quietly**
4. ____ **lovingly**
5. ____ **skillfully**
6. ____ **slyly**
7. ____ **honestly**
8. ____ **very**
9. ____ **almost**
10. ____ **hardly**

a. ably
b. affectionately
c. barely
d. correctly
e. craftily
f. nearly
g. silently
h. gratefully
i. truthfully
j. quite

B. Directions: Complete the crossword puzzle. Clues are synonyms of the answer words. Use the first letters as clues.

ACROSS
3. happily
6. definitely
8. entirely

DOWN
1. rarely
2. legibly
4. truly
5. forever
7. approximately

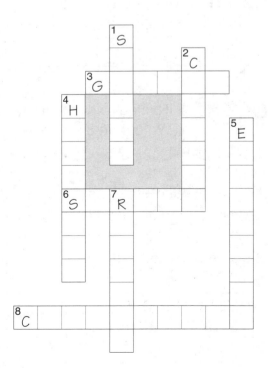

Name: _____ Date: _____

SYNONYMS: ADVERBS 2

Directions: First unscramble the adverb in each sentence. Then circle its synonym.

1. Did you know that yo-yos were
   (STRIF) _____
   used as weapons?

   never   originally

   often   seldom

2. That story you just told is **(TALTOLY)**
   _____ fantastic!

   entirely   partly

   almost   not

3. Gladys's clever new dance steps are **(MYSLIP)** _____ amazing!

   never   hardly   utterly   surprisingly

4. Justin **(NIBLDLY)** _____ joined in with whatever his friends
   were doing.

   happily   sadly   frequently   mindlessly

5. The careless electrician had made a **(YEVR)** _____ foolish error.

   quite   slightly   stupidly   almost

6. Almost **(LACITANCEDYL)** _____, the scientist made a great
   new discovery.

   overnight   immediately   wisely   mistakenly

7. The watermelon that won the contest was **(RETEXEMYL)** _____
   large.

   greatly   slightly   moderately   almost

8. An **(SULALUNUY)** _____ fast car passed us on the freeway.

   barely   remarkably   hardly   dangerously

Name: _____   **Date:** _____

Building Vocabulary Skills and Strategies, Level 7 • Saddleback Publishing, Inc. ©2004 • 3 Watson, Irvine, CA 92618 • Phone (888) SDL-BACK • www.sdlback.com   63

ANTONYMS: NOUNS 1

The artful use of *antonyms—words* with opposite meanings—can make your meanings crystal clear.

A. **Directions:** Draw a line to match each **boldface** noun with its antonym.

1. **ally**   a. humility
2. **impatience**   b. calmness
3. **disturbance**   c. enemy
4. **pride**   d. success
5. **destruction**   e. creation
6. **disappointment**   f. patience

7. **endurance**   g. submission
8. **fad**   h. greeting
9. **struggle**   i. weakness
10. **farewell**   j. original
11. **imitation**   k. cruelty
12. **kindness**   l. convention

B. **Directions:** Use vowels *(a, e, i, o, u)* to complete the antonyms of the **boldface** nouns.

1. **laziness** / _v_ _ _g_ _ _r_
2. **leisure** / _t_ _ _ _l_
3. **confusion** / _c_ _l_ _ _r_ _ _t_y_
4. **treason** / _p_ _ _t_r_ _ _ _t_ _ _s_m_

5. **virtue** / _ _v_ _l_
6. **youth** / _m_ _ _t_ _ _r_ _ _t_y_
7. **background** / _f_ _ _r_ _ _g_r_ _ _ _n_d_
8. **seriousness** / _j_ _ _l_l_ _ _t_y_

C. **Directions:** Unscramble the antonyms. Then use each word in a sentence.

1. separation / **(TUINY)** _____: _____
   _____

2. emotion / **(EONRAS)** _____: _____
   _____

3. scoundrel / **(NAGLEMTEN)** _____:_____
   _____

4. prudence / **(SHERSANS)** _____:_____
   _____

Name: _____   **Date:** _____

ANTONYMS: NOUNS 2

A. Directions:
Use the nouns in the box to make 14 pairs of antonyms.

B. Directions:
Complete the crossword puzzle with antonyms of the clue words.

attic	courtesy	disrespect	heroism
cellar	dullness	hesitation	inclusion
brightness	hindrance	injustice	jobless
cowardice	elimination	flabbiness	importance
assistance	decision	employed	laughter
fairness	punishment	triviality	weeping
deflation	firmness	inflation	pardon

ACROSS
2. capture
5. loser
6. obscurity
7. attack

DOWN
1. smoothness
3. prosperity
4. ignorance

1. _____ / _____
2. _____ / _____
3. _____ / _____
4. _____ / _____
5. _____ / _____
6. _____ / _____
7. _____ / _____
8. _____ / _____
9. _____ / _____
10. _____ / _____
11. _____ / _____
12. _____ / _____
13. _____ / _____
14. _____ / _____

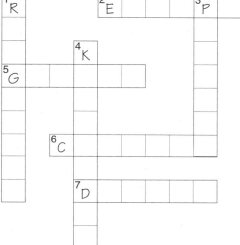

Name: _____ Date: _____

ANTONYMS: VERBS 1

Remember that *verbs* are words that express an action, an occurrence, or a state of being.

Directions: Circle the *antonym* of the **boldface** verb in each sentence.

1. Cynthia decided to **increase** the time she spends practicing ballet.

   enjoy   lengthen   justify   abbreviate

2. The counselor told the young campers to **join** hands.

   hold   wash   disconnect   massage

3. After a long, drawn-out trial, the prisoner was finally **exonerated**.

   convicted   shackled   questioned   honored

4. Stanley bravely tried to **banish** all frightening thoughts from his mind.

   hide   welcome   forget   remember

5. Some people believe that opposites **attract**.

   repel   connect   show off   communicate

6. The babysitter **entertained** the restless little boys for four hours.

   danced   pampered   ignored   watched

7. The rebel forces **imprisoned** their captive for five long months.

   tortured   questioned   nourished   released

8. The condition of the infected tooth gradually **worsened** over the weekend.

   improved   ached   diminished   deteriorated

9. After fitting the new pipe, the plumber **tightened** the bolts.

   sold   attached   loosened   checked

Name: _____   **Date:** _____

66 *Building Vocabulary Skills and Strategies, Level 7* • Saddleback Publishing, Inc. ©2004 • 3 Watson, Irvine, CA 92618 • Phone (888) SDL-BACK • www.sdlback.com

ANTONYMS: VERBS 2

A. Directions: Unscramble the word to complete each pair of *antonyms*.

1. depart / (REAVRI) _____

2. defrost (EREFEZ) _____

3. isolate (NIDCULE) _____

4. resist / (BUSTIM) _____

5. pity / (NEVY) _____

6. evade / (CAPARPHO) _____

7. purchase / (LESL) _____

8. allow / (DIBROF) _____

9. esteem / (COMK) _____

10. display / (OCANCEL) _____

B. Directions: Complete the crossword puzzle with antonyms of the clue words. Use the first letters as clues.

ACROSS
2. flatten
4. agree
7. begin
8. complicate

DOWN
1. soften
3. bore
5. cover
6. fire

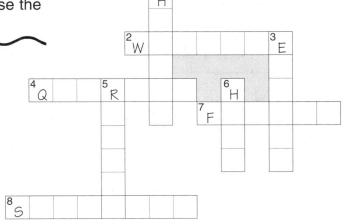

Name: _____ Date: _____

ANTONYMS: ADJECTIVES 1

You already know that *adjectives* describe nouns and pronouns. But do you also know that adjectives often tell *how many* or *what kind*?

A. Directions: Add vowels *(a, e, i, o, u)* to complete the antonyms of the **boldface** adjectives.

1. Casual clothes are all right for regular school dances, but the prom is a
   _f_ _ _r_ _m_ _ _ _l_ affair.

2. That puppy is very active, but this one seems very _p_ _ _ _s_ _s_ _ _ _v_ _.

3. We had to replace the warped board with a _s_ _t_ _r_ _ _ _ _g_ _h_ _t_ one.

4. This undervalued antique was once a little girl's _c_ _h_ _ _ _r_ _ _s_ _h_ _ _d_ doll.

5. Saul was embarrassed about his act at the talent show, but Roger was
   _p_ _r_ _ _ _ _d_ of his.

6. Is Elizabeth's playmate an actual one or an _ _ _m_ _ _g_ _ _n_ _ _r_ _y_ one?

7. We wanted a secluded campsite, but all we could find was a
   _c_ _r_ _ _ _w_ _d_ _ _ _d_ area.

8. The native population resented the influx of the _ _ _l_ _ _ _ _n_ intruders.

B. Directions: Find an antonym in the box for each adjective below. Write it on the line.

bound	comfortable	delicate	elongated	harmless	lowered	optimistic	resistant

1. **yielding** /_____

2. **tough** /_____

3. **shortened** /_____

4. **elevated** /_____

5. **uneasy** /_____

6. **loose** /_____

7. **injurious** /_____

8. **pessimistic** /_____

Name: _____   Date: _____

68 *Building Vocabulary Skills and Strategies, Level 7* • Saddleback Publishing, Inc. ©2004 • 3 Watson, Irvine, CA 92618 • Phone (888) SDL-BACK • www.sdlback.com

ANTONYMS: ADJECTIVES 2

A. Directions: Unscramble the adjectives to complete each pair of *antonyms*.

1. cheerful / **(LOYGOM)** _____

2. internal / **(TENLERAX)** _____

3. rare / **(MOCNOM)** _____

4. original / **(PEDCIO)** _____

5. extended / **(EBIRF)** _____

6. logical / **(LARAINIROT)** _____

7. obedient / **(RULNUY)** _____

8. incompetent / **(LEAB)** _____

9. righteous / **(LETUHICAN)** _____

10. deficient / **(ETAQADUE)** _____

B. Directions: Complete the crossword puzzle with antonyms of the **boldface** clue words.

ACROSS

4. a **lively** participant

6. your **truthful** eyes

7. **dainty** material

DOWN

1. a **generous** fellow

2. the **hydrated** plant

3. **vulgar** manners

5. an **unscrupulous** decision

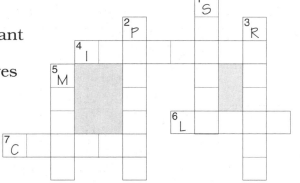

Name: _____ Date: _____

ANTONYMS: ADVERBS 1

Remember that *adverbs* modify verbs, adjectives, or other adverbs.

A. Directions: Find an *antonym* (word that means the opposite) in the box for each **boldface** adverb. Write it on the line. Hint: You will *not* use all the words.

| abruptly | angrily | briskly | unhappily | foolishly |
| accidentally | brightly | certainly | often | thoughtfully |

1. Jeremy said goodbye to Alexis very **slowly** (_____).
2. Janice very **wisely** (_____) refrained from overeating.
3. Emma **seldom** (_____) goes to the movies.
4. Homer looked up **dully** (_____) and said, "Huh?"
5. On hot days, Monica moves very **sluggishly** (_____).
6. When asked if he would get an A on the test, Al said, "**Doubtfully**." (_____).
7. After her long vacation, Amanda **joyfully** (_____) returned home.
8. Dustin **purposely** (_____) turned off the computer.
9. Dana **selfishly** (_____) kept all the good peaches for himself.

B. Directions: Complete the puzzle with antonyms of the **boldface** adverbs.

ACROSS
3. behaves **indifferently**
5. **partly** responsible
6. treated **roughly**
7. acted **sanely**

DOWN
1. **indistinctly** visible
2. **busily** at work
4. greeted **courteously**
5. **unjustly** angry

Name: _____ Date: _____

70 Building Vocabulary Skills and Strategies, Level 7 • Saddleback Publishing, Inc. ©2004 • 3 Watson, Irvine, CA 92618 • Phone (888) SDL-BACK • www.sdlback.com

ANTONYMS: ADVERBS 2

A. Directions: Sort the adverbs in the box to make six pairs of *antonyms* (words with opposite meanings). Write them on the lines. See the example.

angrily	awkwardly	definitely
sometimes	famously	gracefully
commonly	invariably	patiently
obscurely	unusually	questionably

1. *angrily*
   patiently

2. _____

3. _____

4. _____

5. _____

6. _____

B. Directions: Complete the crossword puzzle with antonyms of the **boldface** adverbs. Use the first letters as clues.

ACROSS
1. **Fortunately**, he won.
6. She spoke **sweetly**.
7. He landed the plane **dangerously**.
8. **Sometimes** she danced.
9. They moved **quickly**.

DOWN
2. I treated him **kindly**.
3. Hank spoke **distinctly**.
4. She's **rarely** in a good mood.
5. Sue played **energetically**.

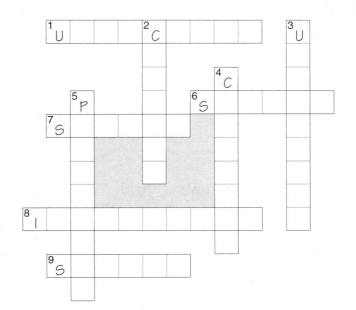

Name: _____   Date: _____

HOMOPHONES

Homophones are words that sound alike but are spelled differently and have different meanings. Some examples of homophones are *be/bee* and *flour/flower*.

A. Directions: Say the words aloud. Then write a homophone next to each word.

1. allowed / _____
2. crews / _____
3. lie / _____
4. ball / _____
5. find / _____
6. meet / _____
7. sent / _____
8. main / _____
9. one / _____

B. Directions: Complete the crossword puzzle with homophones for the **boldface** words.

ACROSS
2. a sincere **compliment**
4. belongs to **him**
5. everyone **who's** here
7. a freshly **mown** lawn
8. **pour** the milk
9. **shoot** the breeze
10. going **away**

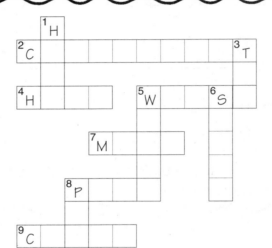

DOWN
1. a **holey** shirt
3. a cup of **tea**
5. all **we've** been doing
6. the lights **shone** brightly
8. a cat's **paws**

C. Directions: Circle three homophone errors in each sentence. Then rewrite the sentences correctly on the lines.

1. The buoy climbed up the fur tree and the beach tree.
   _____

2. After the accident, wee set off fore flairs to get attention.
   _____

Name: _____   Date: _____

HOMOPHONE RIDDLES

You can figure out these riddles by using your imagination and your sense of humor!

EXAMPLE: What would you call a music group that is no longer allowed to play music?   a <u>banned</u> <u>band</u>

A. Directions: Use vowels *(a, e, i, o, u)* to fill in the blanks.

What would you call . . .

1. a poet in jail? b_rr_d b_rd
2. a dog's sound on a boat? b_rq__ b_rk
3. a container for cotton pods? b_ll b_wl
4. a variety of breakfast food day after day? s_r__l c_r__l
5. corn for military higher-ups? k_rn_ls for c_l_n_ls
6. a medieval jouster who doesn't like the daytime? n_ght kn_ght
7. a greeting from someone in a hot-air balloon? a h_gh h_

B. Directions: Now solve the riddles by using only the first letters as clues.

What would you call . . .

1. a monk who cooks chicken? f_____ f_____
2. an unfriendly, cheap youth hotel? h_____ h_____
3. a dish full of supplies for making braids? p_____ p_____
4. a seer who tells the future for money? p_____ for p_____
5. a colorless bucket? p_____ p_____
6. a picturesque view that was observed? s_____ s_____

HOMOGRAPHS

Words that are spelled alike but have different meanings are called *homographs*.

EXAMPLE: *baste* 1. to pour liquid on while roasting; 2. to sew with long stitches

A. Directions: Unscramble the homographs that match each definition below. The first one has been done for you.

1. (TUCERON) __counter__:
   a. one who counts
   b. long table in a store or restaurant

2. (INEP) _____:
   a. to yearn or long for
   b. a type of evergreen

3. (MODCUNOP) _____:
   a. having more than one part
   b. an enclosed yard

4. (WOBL) _____:
   a. a hard hit
   b. send forth a stream of air

5. (ENFI) _____:
   a. high quality
   b. money paid as punishment

6. (DEHI) _____:
   a. to conceal; keep out of sight
   b. animal skin

B. Directions: Write homographs to find the answer to the riddle (reads top to bottom). Use the definitions as clues. The first one has been done for you.

RIDDLE: *Homographs have the same spelling but different meanings and _____.*

1. bubbling of hot liquid; red swelling on the skin   1. b o i l
2. container made of glass; to rattle or vibrate   2. _ _ _ _
3. container for pouring liquid; baseball player   3. _ _ _ _ _ _
4. one side of a sheet of paper; youth who runs errands   4. _ _ _ _
5. friendly and helpful; same type or class   5. _ _ _ _
6. opposite of *up*; soft feathers   6. _ _ _ _
7. newly made, not stale; impudent, bold   7. _ _ _ _ _

Name: _____   Date: _____

HOMOPHONES AND HOMOGRAPHS: DICTIONARY PRACTICE

Remember these definitions:
- *Homophones* are words that <u>sound</u> exactly alike but have different spellings and meanings.
- *Homographs* are words that <u>look</u> exactly alike but have <u>different</u> meanings.

A. Directions: First write the *homophone* for each **boldface** word. Then write a brief definition of the homophone you added. Check a dictionary if you need help.

1. Sheila has a new **beau**. _____ : _____

2. The ref **blew** the whistle. _____ : _____

3. Hal removed the apple **core**. _____ : _____

4. The horses ate **hay**. _____ : _____

5. The **lesson** took 50 minutes. _____ : _____

B. Directions: Write two sentences showing each meaning of the **boldface** *homographs*. The first one has been done for you. Check a dictionary if you need help.

1. **carp** (verb) *If you carp about something, you complain about it.*
   carp (noun) *A carp is an edible fish found in fresh water.*

2. **chuck** (noun) _____
   chuck (verb) _____

3. **hatch** (noun) _____
   hatch (verb) _____

Name: _____ Date: _____

CLIPPED WORDS 1

A "clipped" word is one that has been shortened by common use, such as "trike" instead of "tricycle."

A. Directions: Write out the complete form of the clipped words shown in **boldface**. Check a dictionary if you're not sure.

1. buy a new **auto** _____

2. a young **coed** _____

3. the study of **trig** _____

4. a **deli** sandwich _____

5. one **cent** in change _____

6. a **cuke** for your salad _____

7. go underwater in a **sub** _____

8. wear a **wig** _____

B. Directions: Now write the clipped form of each **boldface** word or words.

1. a talented **veterinarian** _____

2. a **typographical** error _____

3. go out to **luncheon** _____

4. an attractive **debutante** _____

5. see the **doctor** _____

6. a **modern** hair style _____

7. wearing tailored **pantaloons** _____

8. an arrangement of **chrysanthemums** _____

Name: _____ Date: _____

CLIPPED WORDS 2

A. Directions: Solve the crossword puzzle. Answers are the complete forms of the **boldface** clipped words.

ACROSS
3. wore a tie and **tails**
4. told the pest to **scram**
5. brewed in a **still**
6. wore thick **specs**
7. coffee began to **perk**

DOWN
1. **lube** the engine
2. sit around and **gab**

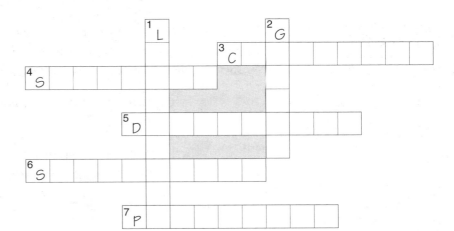

B. Directions: Use vowels (a, e, i, o, u) to complete the longer form of each **boldface** clipped word.

1. The only job Jacob could get was as a taxicab **hack**. h _ c k n _ y

2. Barbara bought a new **curio** cabinet. c _ r _ _ s _ t y

3. Larry went to see a **movie**. m _ v _ n g p _ c t _ r _

4. The criminal had spent many years in the **pen**.
   p _ n _ t _ n t _ _ r y

5. Theresa drove 40 miles on the **pike**. t _ r n p _ k _

6. Donald is on the **varsity** football team. _ n _ v _ r s _ t y

7. Caroline and Richard went to the **prom** together. p r _ m _ n _ d _

WORDS BORROWED FROM NAMES 1

Many English words had their origins in the names of people and places. For example, *cashmere*, a fine wool fabric, is named for the goats of Kashmir, India, whose downy wool is used in the manufacture of this product.

A. Directions: Write a letter to match each **boldface** word with its origin.

1. _____ **argyle**
2. _____ **cologne**
3. _____ **doily**
4. _____ **frankfurter**
5. _____ **manila paper**
6. _____ **quisling**
7. _____ **sandwich**
8. _____ **suede**

a. named after the Scottish clan Campbell of Argyll, Scotland

b. named by the French after the Swedish inventor of this type of leather

c. named for the German city of Cologne, which in turn was named after Colonia Agrippina, the Roman empress who was born there

d. named after the hemp made in Manila, the Philippines, from which it was originally made

e. named after Vidkun Quisling, a Norwegian who was shot for treason after World War II

f. named after the city of Frankfurt, Germany

g. named after John Montagu, fourth Earl of Sandwich, who invented it so he could continue gambling without stopping for a normal meal

h. named for a person named Doily or Doyley, who kept a shop in London in the late 17th century

B. Directions: Look up the origins of these words and write them on the lines.

1. **tabby** _____
2. **martinet** _____
3. **diesel** _____
4. **dunce** _____
5. **guillotine** _____

WORDS BORROWED FROM NAMES 2

The names of places, people, and even gods form the basis of many English words.

Directions: Use the clues to complete the crossword puzzle.

ACROSS

3. Amelia Bloomer, a pioneer feminist, made this garment popular.
5. Atlas was a Titan in Greek myth. In the front of books of maps, he was often pictured holding up the earth.
6. A man named Beaulieu, a famous hatter of the mid-19th century, designed this hat that has a low crown.
11. Louis Pasteur invented the process by which we do this to our milk to kill bacteria.
12. This day of the week is named after Fria, the Norse goddess of love and beauty.

DOWN

1. This month is named after Julius Caesar.
2. These crackers are named after their inventor, Sylvester Graham. (2 words)
4. Samuel Maverick, a Texan who didn't brand his cattle, gives us this word for someone who doesn't follow the crowd.
7. Teddy Roosevelt was the U.S. president who spared the life of a bear cub on a hunting trip in Mississippi. (2 words)
8. The Italian physicist Alessandro Volta named this unit for measuring the force of an electrical current.
9. This soft knitted cloth was originally made in Jersey, a British island in the English Channel.
10. This month was named for the Roman goddess Maia.

Name: _____ Date: _____

FOREIGN WORDS AND PHRASES 1

Many words and phrases from other languages have found their way into the English language.

Directions: Use context clues to help you figure out the meaning of the **boldface** words and phrases. Check a dictionary if you need help. Circle a letter to show your answer.

1. "**Entre nous**," said Yvonne as a warning to Emma to keep the information secret.
   a. or else
   b. now or never
   c. between ourselves

2. When Allison saw the **trompe-l'oeil** design on the wall, she thought she was looking down a long hallway.
   a. optical illusion
   b. checkerboard
   c. oil paint

3. Ross purchased a **pied-à-terre** so he wouldn't have to pay hotel bills when he visited the city.
   a. minivan with television monitors
   b. apartment maintained for convenience
   c. hotel pass good for a year

4. Andy had a moment of **déjà vu**. "I know we've met before," he said.
   a. a feeling that something strange is about to happen
   b. the illusion of having experienced something previously
   c. the wish to impress strangers

5. The **crudités** served at the party were healthful in themselves, but the dips were full of fat.
   a. raw vegetables
   b. chips
   c. drinks

6. Vincent was proud to see his name included in the **dramatis personae** of the play.
   a. advertisers
   b. cast of characters
   c. stagehands and assistants

7. This wonderful weather seems to invite us to dine **al fresco**.
   a. on light food
   b. in a leisurely manner
   c. outdoors

A-B WORDS IN CONTEXT 2

Directions: Read the definitions of the A-B words. Then use each word in an original sentence.

accuracy freedom from all errors or mistakes

acknowledge to recognize the authority or claims of

adjourn to stop a meeting, etc. with the intention of beginning again later

affinity a natural attraction or liking

banish to force to leave a country, as by political decree

blackmail to get money or a service from, by threatening to tell something damaging

boundary something, as a line or mark, that forms an outer limit, edge, or extent

bureaucracy government with many departments made up of appointed officials, who follow set rules and regulations

buttress a structure built against a wall to strengthen it

1. _____
2. _____
3. _____
4. _____
5. _____
6. _____
7. _____
8. _____
9. _____

Name: _____ Date: _____

C-D WORDS IN CONTEXT 1

Now let's learn some C-D words that could *develop* your vocabulary very *creatively*.

Directions: Complete the sentences with words from the box. Hint: You will *not* use all the words. Check a dictionary if you need help.

cabaret

carbonated

civilian

cognizant

commuter

credence

custody

dahlia

defiance

depreciate

dexterity

disguise

dubious

1. Bob's silly _____ didn't fool anyone.

2. After 20 years in the army, Robert is now looking forward to _____ life.

3. Ginger's favorite _____ drink is ginger ale.

4. After reading the warning about jellyfish, I was _____ about going into the water.

5. Percy would rather go to a _____ than a regular restaurant because he enjoys the entertainment.

6. Samantha arranged a bouquet with irises, tulips, daffodils, and one perfect red _____.

7. Since Tim had always been so trustworthy, it was easy to put _____ in his unlikely story.

8. The willful child's _____ of the rules led to his expulsion from school.

9. The currency of that country continued to _____ for months.

10. The foster parents have had _____ of the child since December.

11. The juggler demonstrated great _____ when he juggled a bowling ball, a baseball, and a grapefruit.

12. The president was _____ of the situation, but he was powerless to do anything.

Name: _____   **Date:** _____

92   *Building Vocabulary Skills and Strategies, Level 7* • Saddleback Publishing, Inc. ©2004 • 3 Watson, Irvine, CA 92618 • Phone (888) SDL-BACK • www.sdlback.com

C-D WORDS IN CONTEXT 2

Directions: Read the definitions of the C-D words. Then use each word in an original sentence.

chafe to make or become rough or sore by rubbing

chignon a tight ball or roll of hair women wear at the back of the head

consequences results or effects

correspond to write or exchange letters

debtor a person who owes something to another, such as money or services

dilemma your position when faced with two poor choices

diversity variety

dormant asleep, or as if asleep

dwindle to become steadily smaller or less; to shrink

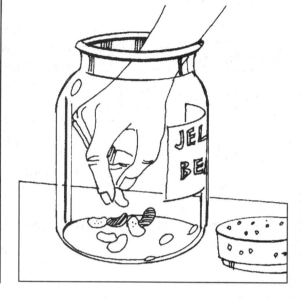

1. _____
2. _____
3. _____
4. _____
5. _____
6. _____
7. _____
8. _____
9. _____

Name: _____ Date: _____

E-F WORDS IN CONTEXT 1

Try adding some E-F words to your vocabulary to give it a little more *élan* and *flair*.

Directions: Complete the sentences with words from the box. Hint: You will *not* use all the words. Check a dictionary if you need help.

Word Box:
- earnest
- ecstasy
- elaborate
- emulate
- escapade
- exceed
- fallible
- fauna
- firmament
- flaunt
- forfeit
- forlorn
- fragment
- froth

1. Brandon's latest _____ resulted in two broken bones and a wrecked car.

2. Charles is often annoying, especially when he wants to _____ his knowledge of local history.

3. Flavio delivered a sincere and _____ apology to Misty.

4. If you _____ the speed limit, you are likely to get a traffic ticket.

5. Instead of using the word *sky* in her poem, Felicia used the word _____ to mean the same thing.

6. Don't believe everything Lester says, because, like all human beings, he is _____.

7. One _____ of the broken mirror remained hidden in the corner.

8. The _____ dinner Carmen prepared for her friends began with very tasty appetizers.

9. The _____ of that area includes deer, squirrels, bobcats, woodpeckers, and lizards.

10. When Clara blew out through the straw, a _____ formed on top of her root beer float.

11. You will be in _____ when you taste Chef Pierre's latest creation.

12. Young actors today often _____ the macho style of the young Marlon Brando.

Name: _____ Date: _____

94 Building Vocabulary Skills and Strategies, Level 7 • Saddleback Publishing, Inc. ©2004 • 3 Watson, Irvine, CA 92618 • Phone (888) SDL-BACK • www.sdlback.com

E-F WORDS IN CONTEXT 2

Directions: Read the definitions of the E-F words. Then use each word in an original sentence.

ebullient bubbling over with high spirits and enthusiasm

edifice a building, especially a large and impressive structure

eloquence moving and skillful use of language, especially in speaking

equator an imaginary line that encircles the earth exactly halfway between the North Pole and the South Pole

estimate to make a close guess as to size, number, cost, etc.

exclude to keep out or shut out

faucet a device with an adjustable valve used to regulate the flow of a liquid, as from a pipe

fickle likely to change without warning; not constant in feeling, purpose, or nature

flamingo a pink or red wading bird that lives in tropical areas and has a long neck and long legs

flourish to grow vigorously; thrive

1. _____
2. _____
3. _____
4. _____
5. _____
6. _____
7. _____
8. _____
9. _____
10. _____

Name: _____   **Date:** _____

G-H WORDS IN CONTEXT 1

Learning some impressive words like *grandiloquent* can add some *heft* to your vocabulary.

Directions: Complete the sentences with words from the box. Hint: You will *not* use all the words. Check a dictionary if you need help.

gallant

garment

genuflect

goblet

grandiose

grimace

guilty

harvest

headquarters

hearth

heritage

homage

hypothetical

1. His dislocated shoulder caused Keith to _____ in pain.

2. I'd rather drink this beverage from a mug than from a _____.

3. In some churches, it is customary to _____ before entering a pew.

4. In the Middle Ages, vassals paid _____ to lords in exchange for protection.

5. Our town's police _____ is located at the corner of Fifth and Main.

6. Sylvia stored her fireplace tools on the raised _____ in the family room.

7. The furnishings in the _____ mansion were carved from the finest woods.

8. The _____ young man held the door open for his mother.

9. The _____ of the Irish includes fiddle music and dancing the jig.

10. We look forward to the fall _____ when all the apples ripen.

11. You'll enjoy wearing this _____ because it's made of the finest silk.

Name: _____ **Date:** _____

96 *Building Vocabulary Skills and Strategies, Level 7* • Saddleback Publishing, Inc. ©2004 • 3 Watson, Irvine, CA 92618 • Phone (888) SDL-BACK • www.sdlback.com

G-H WORDS IN CONTEXT 2

Directions: Read the definitions of the G-H words. Then use each word in an original sentence.

gallop the fastest gait of a four-footed animal

gazpacho a chilled soup made of tomatoes, spices, and other vegetables

glut too great a supply of something

goulash a stew of beef or veal with vegetables and paprika and other spices

gratifying giving pleasure or satisfaction

haggle to argue about the price of something

hazard a dangerous or perilous situation

heap a collection of things arranged in a pile

helmet a protective covering for the head

hurdle a small frame or fence to be jumped over in a race

1. _____
2. _____
3. _____
4. _____
5. _____
6. _____
7. _____
8. _____
9. _____
10. _____

Name: _____   Date: _____

I-J WORDS IN CONTEXT 1

You would be *imprudent*, or lacking in *judgment*, if you failed to add these I-J words to your vocabulary.

Directions: Complete the sentences with words from the box. Hint: You will *not* use all the words. Check a dictionary if you need help.

| identical | illusion | inconsistent | inexpensive | inhale | insomnia | itemize |
| jaguar | jargon | jiggle | jog | jumbo | jungle | juvenile |

1. A _____ is a large, spotted wild cat resembling a leopard.

2. A lush oasis is an optical _____ often seen in a desert.

3. Because these dresses are so _____, I think I'll buy several of them.

4. The door will open if you _____ the key in the lock a little bit.

5. Many types of animals are found only in the tropical _____.

6. Pedro couldn't finish the _____ ice cream cone before it started to melt.

7. The lawyers spoke in their own _____, making it difficult for anyone else to understand them.

8. The purses look _____, so how can I tell which one is a designer original?

9. The suspect's story was _____ from one day to the next.

10. This type of motion picture appeals mainly to a _____ audience.

11. When breathing, it's important to _____ deeply.

Name: _____ Date: _____

I-J WORDS IN CONTEXT 2

Directions: Read the definitions of the I-J words. Then use each word in an original sentence.

ideology the ideas or beliefs held by a class or group

inaugurate to install in an office with a formal ceremony

indigestion the inability to digest food, or difficulty in digesting food

infancy the time of being a baby

innovation a change in the usual way of doing things

janitor a person hired to clean and take care of a building

jest something said or done to provoke laughter; joke

jubilant joyful and proud

junction a point at which things meet or join

justice the quality of being fair and impartial

1. _____
2. _____
3. _____
4. _____
5. _____
6. _____
7. _____
8. _____
9. _____
10. _____

Name: _____ Date: _____

K-L WORDS IN CONTEXT 1

It's not all that *laborious* to add to your *knowledge* of K-L words—so let's get started!

Directions: Complete the sentences with words from the box. Hint: You will *not* use all the words. Check a dictionary if you need help.

kaleidoscope
keg
kernel
kindle
kiosk
kosher
lacquer
languid
ledge
leisure
lenient
literacy
lopsided

1. A child's first step toward achieving _____ is learning the alphabet.

2. We need every _____ of corn from these cobs to make the corn chowder.

3. In Patrick's _____ time, he likes to do crossword puzzles.

4. Mr. Porter buys his morning newspaper at the _____ on the corner.

5. Once we applied _____ to the table, it was as shiny as the rest of the furniture.

6. The beginner made a vase in her ceramics class, but it turned out a bit _____.

7. The ever-changing patterns made by a _____ became the subject of the artist's paintings.

8. The hot weather had us all feeling quite _____ and slightly grumpy.

9. The only kind of pickles Tom will eat are _____ dills.

10. This wooden _____ holds 10 gallons of apple cider.

11. We have to _____ these small pieces of wood to get the campfire started.

Name: _____ **Date:** _____

100 *Building Vocabulary Skills and Strategies, Level 7* • Saddleback Publishing, Inc. ©2004 • 3 Watson, Irvine, CA 92618 • Phone (888) SDL-BACK • www.sdlback.com

K-L WORDS IN CONTEXT 2

Directions: Read the definitions of the K-L words. Then use each word in an original sentence.

kangaroo an Australian animal, the female of which carries the young in a pouch

kelp a coarse, brown seaweed

keyboard the row or rows of keys, as in a piano or a computer

kinship relationship, especially by blood

kumquat a sour, tangy citrus fruit resembling a tiny orange

landmark a hill, tree, etc. used to recognize a place

ledge a shelf, sill, or other surface jutting out from a wall or window

liquefy to make or become liquid

loiter to linger or dawdle

luxury anything costly but unnecessary that gives comfort or pleasure, but is not necessary to life or health

1. _____
2. _____
3. _____
4. _____
5. _____
6. _____
7. _____
8. _____
9. _____
10. _____

Name: _____ Date: _____

M-N WORDS IN CONTEXT 1

Don't *neglect* these M-N words! If you study them well, you'll remove all *mystery* about their meanings.

Directions: Complete the sentences with words from the box. Hint: You will *not* use all the words. Check a dictionary if you need help.

mahogany	martyr	menace	mildew	modem	mortality	muffin
naive	necessary	nobility	nomadic	nonchalant	nozzle	nudge

1. A _____ is someone who will suffer or die rather than give up his or her beliefs.

2. As a member of a _____ tribe, Ahmed moved constantly in search of food.

3. Beatrice is _____ if she believes every salesperson's claims.

4. Dominick needs to get a _____ so he can hook up to the Internet.

5. Grace usually has a blueberry _____ and some tea for breakfast.

6. Isabel gave Clara a little _____ to get her attention.

7. Keith needs to replace the _____ on his garden hose.

8. _____ developed in the damp closet, ruining many of Maxine's clothes.

9. Sadie couldn't decide between teak and _____ for her new furniture.

10. That vicious criminal is a _____ to society!

11. The crowd was excited, but the quarterback seemed almost _____ about the victory.

12. Your help on this project is absolutely _____ to our success.

Name: _____   **Date:** _____

102 *Building Vocabulary Skills and Strategies, Level 7* • Saddleback Publishing, Inc. ©2004 • 3 Watson, Irvine, CA 92618 • Phone (888) SDL-BACK • www.sdlback.com

M-N WORDS IN CONTEXT 2

Directions: Read the definitions of the M-N words. Then use each word in an original sentence.

macaroni hollow pasta tubes often baked with cheese
manipulate to operate or work with the hands; handle
matriarch female ruler or head, as of her family, tribe, or community
miser a greedy, stingy person who hoards money instead of using it
mysterious impossible or difficult to explain or understand
navigation the art of charting the position and course of a ship or aircraft
neutral not on one side or the other in a dispute, contest, or war
notify to give notice to; to inform

nourish to keep alive and healthy by feeding
nugget a lump, especially of gold in its natural state

1. _____
2. _____
3. _____
4. _____
5. _____
6. _____
7. _____
8. _____
9. _____
10. _____

Name: _____   Date: _____

O-P WORDS IN CONTEXT 1

You can't be *overly prepared* for vocabulary tests.
So add these O-P words to your list.

Directions: Complete the sentences with words from the box. Hint: You will *not* use all the words. Check a dictionary if you need help.

obituary	octave	omnivorous	ordeal	original
ottoman	overalls	pagan	patriarch	pedicure
phantom	plateau	posture	prize	purpose

1. Aaron stands up so straight he could be a model for good _____.

2. As _____ of the family, Murray was responsible for 14 people.

3. Carla sang the song a full _____ higher than James did.

4. Gloria chooses a different nail polish color every time she gets a _____.

5. By nature humans are _____ creatures, but some people prefer to be herbivorous.

6. Jessica's _____ began when she got lost in the forest.

7. Ms. Jefferson's _____ said that she had lived for 93 years.

8. Although it was an accident, Sherri thought Colleen had tripped her on _____.

9. That brown _____ does not look right with the black chair.

10. The _____ for best apple pie went to Amos this year.

11. The scary story told of a _____ ship that seemed to appear every December.

12. You need the _____ sales receipt to return something to the store.

Name: _____ **Date:** _____

104 *Building Vocabulary Skills and Strategies, Level 7* • Saddleback Publishing, Inc. ©2004 • 3 Watson, Irvine, CA 92618 • Phone (888) SDL-BACK • www.sdlback.com

O-P WORDS IN CONTEXT 2

Directions: Read the definitions of the O-P words. Then use each word in an original sentence.

obscurity the condition of being hidden or unknown

official a person who holds an office or position, as in the government or a business

opposition the act of being against something; resistance

outskirts the outer edges or areas far from the center, as of a city

oxygen a colorless, tasteless, odorless gaseous element making up about a fifth of the earth's atmosphere

parka a fur or cloth jacket, or a coat with a hood

pillar a slender, firm, upright structure of stone, wood, or other material

plunder to rob of goods or property by force; to loot

prescription a physician's formula for preparing and ordering a medicine

prowl to roam about quietly and slyly, as in search of food or something to steal

1. _____

_____

_____

2. _____

_____

3. _____

_____

4. _____

_____

5. _____

_____

6. _____

_____

7. _____

_____

8. _____

_____

9. _____

_____

10. _____

_____

Name: _____   **Date:** _____

Building Vocabulary Skills and Strategies, Level 7 • Saddleback Publishing, Inc. ©2004 • 3 Watson, Irvine, CA 92618 • Phone (888) SDL-BACK • www.sdlback.com   105

Q-R WORDS IN CONTEXT 1

Quick! Run! Let's hurry to learn these Q-R words.

Directions: Complete the sentences with words from the box. Hint: You will *not* use all the words. Check a dictionary if you need help.

quad	quake	queasy	quell	quince
quite	quota	rampage	redeem	repent
reverse	rote	rouse	rupture	

1. Did the criminal ever _____ for the suffering he caused that family?

2. Gladys makes jelly from the fruit of the _____ tree in her yard.

3. If the rebels don't stop their activities, the government will move in to _____ the revolt.

4. At lunchtime, Mickey met Jean in the center of the _____.

5. Sally plans to _____ her coupons for a new toaster oven.

6. The club met its _____ of magazine sales.

7. When it was left alone too long, the dog went on a _____ in the yard.

8. The _____ lasted only 30 seconds, but it did tremendous damage.

9. There's a picture of a building on the _____ side of that coin.

10. Sam feels a little _____ whenever he reads in a moving car.

11. That awful smell was caused by a _____ in a gas line.

Name: _____   **Date:** _____

Q-R WORDS IN CONTEXT 2

Directions: Read the definitions of the Q–R words. Then use each word in an original sentence.

quarantine the isolation of persons exposed to contagious diseases

quart a measure of liquid volume equal to 32 ounces, two pints, or 1/4 gallon

quaver to tremble or shake in an uncertain way, as a voice

quiz a short or informal test given to a student or students

quotient the number that results if one number is divided by another

radius a straight line from the center of a circle or sphere to the circumference or surface

reap to cut down or gather in (grain); harvest (a crop)

regret to feel sorrow or grief about something

resist to work or strive against; oppose

ripple to form into small waves

1. _____

2. _____

3. _____

4. _____

5. _____

6. _____

7. _____

8. _____

9. _____

10. _____

Name: _____ **Date:** _____

Building Vocabulary Skills and Strategies, Level 7 • Saddleback Publishing, Inc. ©2004 • 3 Watson, Irvine, CA 92618 • Phone (888) SDL-BACK • www.sdlback.com 107

S-T WORDS IN CONTEXT 1

Do you have the *temerity* to learn and use these S-T words in your everyday vocabulary? If so, that's just *swell*!

Directions: Complete the sentences with words from the box. Hint: You will *not* use all the words. Check a dictionary if you need help.

sacrifice
segment
silhouette
smear
spare
stiff
swelter
tactful
temerity
temper
thorn
tortoise
triceps
tyranny

1. After taking assertiveness lessons, Jake finally had the _____ to ask for a raise.

2. It wasn't very _____ to ask June about the breakup with her boyfriend.

3. Dennis was developing his _____ by working out at the gym.

4. Giving up dessert for a month was a great _____ for Gina.

5. You will _____ the paint if you touch it before it dries.

6. Marlene's painfully _____ neck prevented her from driving.

7. Mr. Chavez has been in a good _____ since his business improved.

8. Alex carefully cut out a _____ of Abraham Lincoln.

9. The record-breaking heat caused all of us to _____ the entire weekend.

10. The _____ tire came in very handy when we had a flat.

11. There's a particularly large _____ on the stem of this rose.

12. Walter eagerly watched the third _____ of the five-part series.

Name: _____ **Date:** _____

108 *Building Vocabulary Skills and Strategies, Level 7* • Saddleback Publishing, Inc. ©2004 • 3 Watson, Irvine, CA 92618 • Phone (888) SDL-BACK • www.sdlback.com

S-T WORDS IN CONTEXT 2

Directions: Read the definitions of the S-T words. Then use each word in an original sentence.

scheme a plan or plot, especially one that's secret and sly
shield to protect or guard
squadron in the U.S. Navy, a group or unit of vessels or aircraft
subtle not direct or obvious; hard to see or understand
syrup a thick, sweet liquid, as that made by boiling sugar with a liquid
tantalize to tease by offering something and then holding it back
thirst dryness in the mouth and throat caused by a need to drink
tithe a tax or offering of 10 percent of one's income to support a church
transform to greatly change the form or appearance of

tusk a long, pointed, projecting tooth, generally one of a pair, as in the elephant

1. _____
2. _____
3. _____
4. _____
5. _____
6. _____
7. _____
8. _____
9. _____
10. _____

Name: _____ **Date:** _____

U-V WORDS IN CONTEXT 1

Exercise your *vocal* cords by *utilizing* these U-V words in your oral vocabulary.

Directions: Complete the sentences with words from the box. Hint: You will *not* use all the words. Check a dictionary if you need help.

ulcer
unaccompanied
undisciplined
unkempt
unsound
uptown
utter
valid
varnish
venture
vestment
vicinity
vivid
vulgar

1. After stripping and sanding the floors, we applied a clear _____.

2. An _____ minor must be met by someone after a flight.

3. Despite her mother's efforts to keep her clean, Monica always seemed _____.

4. Marsha suffers from a very painful stomach _____.

5. Pamela makes a poor impression because she wears _____ clothing styles.

6. Robert has a _____ imagination, which is useful in his career as a writer.

7. The _____ puppy was making life miserable for the fussy family.

8. Her restaurant is located in the _____ of the downtown park.

9. Felicia's _____ plan has no chance of succeeding.

10. This coupon is _____ only until August 15.

11. When our flashlights failed, we were surrounded by _____ darkness.

Name: _____   **Date:** _____

U-V WORDS IN CONTEXT 2

Directions: Read the definitions of the U-V words. Then use each word in an original sentence.

umiak a large, open Native Alaskan boat, made of skins drawn over a wooden frame

undefeated not defeated or conquered

ungrateful lacking gratitude; not thankful

unpopular not liked or approved of by a rather large number of people

untidy not orderly or neat; messy

vandal person who is willfully destructive

velocity rate of motion or speed

verify to prove to be true or accurate; to confirm

vim force or vigor; energy; spirit

violence force used to cause injury or damage

1. _____

_____

_____

2. _____

_____

3. _____

_____

4. _____

_____

5. _____

_____

6. _____

_____

7. _____

_____

8. _____

_____

9. _____

_____

10. _____

_____

Name: _____   **Date:** _____

W-X WORDS IN CONTEXT 1

You don't need *X-ray* vision to see how *worthwhile* it would be to add these W-X words to your vocabulary.

Directions: Complete the sentences with words from the box. Hint: You will *not* use all the words. Check a dictionary if you need help.

wad	**wade**	**wallet**	**warble**	**waylay**	**wharf**
whiff	**X-axis**	**xenophobe**	**xerography**	**xerothermic**	**xylem**

1. As Wendy walked past the jasmine blossoms, she got a _____ of their aroma.

2. Dorian labeled the _____ on her graph, using very neat numbers.

3. Few plants were able to survive during that _____ period.

4. It's too bad that Oscar is a _____, because he misses out on some interesting friendships.

5. Jan enjoyed going down to the _____ to eat lunch by the bay.

6. Lottie always liked to keep a small _____ of cash tucked away in her purse.

7. The water was shallow enough for us to _____ to the other side.

8. _____ is found in the stems or trunk of a plant.

9. This machine uses the process of _____ to make photocopies.

10. Vic forgot his _____, so his friend had to pay for his dinner.

11. We were awakened each morning by the _____ of a lovely bird.

Name: _____   **Date:** _____

112 *Building Vocabulary Skills and Strategies, Level 7* • Saddleback Publishing, Inc. ©2004 • 3 Watson, Irvine, CA 92618 • Phone (888) SDL-BACK • www.sdlback.com

W-X WORDS IN CONTEXT 2

Directions: Read the definitions of the W-X words. Then use each word in an original sentence.

wafer a thin, crisp biscuit
wasteland a barren, desolate area
weld joining (pieces of metal) by heating or pressing
whimper to cry with low, mournful, broken sounds
wreath a woven ring of flowers or leaves
xanthic yellow or yellowish
xebec a small, three-masted vessel, once used by Algerian pirates in the Mediterranean Sea
xeric having to do with or adapted to a very dry environment
xeriscape a landscape design that relies on little or no water
xerophyte a plant adapted to growing and surviving in a dry environment

1. _____
2. _____
3. _____
4. _____
5. _____
6. _____
7. _____
8. _____
9. _____
10. _____

Name: _____ Date: _____

Y-Z WORDS IN CONTEXT 1

You don't have to be a word *zealot* to say *yes* to learning these Y-Z words. Anyone can do it!

Directions: Complete the sentences with words from the box. Hint: You will *not* use all the words. Check a dictionary if you need help.

yacht

yam

yearling

yelp

yoga

yogurt

youth

zealot

zenith

zeppelin

zinnia

zodiac

zori

1. Bruce often has _____ and granola for breakfast.

2. The _____ has lived at the animal preserve since its birth.

3. Gwyneth rolled up her _____ mat after the 4:00 class concluded.

4. Marvin wants to buy a _____ when he earns his first million.

5. Olivia would rather have a _____ than a baked potato.

6. The signs of the _____ are used in the practice of astrology.

7. The wild-eyed _____ tried to convince us to read his book.

8. When Martha tripped over the dog, the poor animal let out a loud _____.

9. During her final worldwide tour, the singer was at the _____ of her popularity.

10. After the strap on her _____ broke, Shirley's foot burned on the hot sand.

11. Zeke's _____ garden is the most colorful flower garden on the block.

Name: _____   **Date:** _____

114 *Building Vocabulary Skills and Strategies, Level 7* • Saddleback Publishing, Inc. ©2004 • 3 Watson, Irvine, CA 92618 • Phone (888) SDL-BACK • www.sdlback.com

Y-Z WORDS IN CONTEXT 2

Directions: Read the definitions of the Y-Z words. Then use each word in an original sentence.

yahoo a brutish or crude person

yawn to open the mouth wide with a long intake of breath, as when sleepy or bored

yeast a substance used in bread-making that allows the dough to rise

yodel to sing in the form of a warble, with rapid voice changes from normal to a shrill falsetto

yoke a curved, wooden frame that joins two animals, such as oxen

zeal great interest and devotion; enthusiasm

zebra a striped animal related to the horse

zephyr any soft, gentle wind

zest keen enjoyment; great pleasure

zoom to move with a low-pitched but loud humming sound

1. _____

2. _____

3. _____

4. _____

5. _____

6. _____

7. _____

8. _____

9. _____

10. _____

Name: _____   Date: _____

Building Vocabulary Skills and Strategies, Level 7 • Saddleback Publishing, Inc. ©2004 • 3 Watson, Irvine, CA 92618 • Phone (888) SDL-BACK • www.sdlback.com   115

JUST FOR FUN: EXPLAINING WHY OR WHY NOT

Have some fun with these questions that explore your knowledge of some interesting words.

Directions: Check a dictionary to help you answer the questions.

1. Why would a **fakir** be unlikely to wear a **fedora**?
   _____
   _____

2. Would it be easier to study the moon at its **perigee** or at its **apogee**? Why?
   _____
   _____

3. Why would it amaze everyone to see an **ascetic** attired in **silk**?
   _____
   _____

4. Why would it not be surprising to see a **buccaneer** on a **brigantine**?
   _____
   _____

5. Why would an **impostor** travel **incognito**?
   _____
   _____

6. Would you rather have a necklace of **lodestones** or **rhinestones**? Why?
   _____
   _____

7. Why would a railroad worker be more likely to use a **semaphore** than a **metaphor**? Why?
   _____
   _____

8. Would you be more likely to ride a **jennet** or a **jenny**? Why?
   _____
   _____

Name: _____ **Date:** _____

JUST FOR FUN: EXPLORING BIG WORDS

Have some fun with big words as you build your vocabulary!

Directions: Check the dictionary definitions of the **boldface** words to help you answer the questions.

1. Would a teacher be more likely to use **legerdemain** or a **lectern**? Explain your answer. _____

2. Would you rather be regarded as someone full of **rectitude** or **iniquity**? Why? _____

3. Would it be more dangerous to spend time with a **bellicose** person or a **comatose** person? Explain your answer. _____

4. Whom would you rather have as a friend—a **loquacious** person or a **mendacious** person? Why? _____

5. What would make more sense for a recovering patient—a **reversible** bed or an **adjustable** bed? Why? _____

6. Would you be more likely to see a **bobolink** in a **metropolitan** or **agrarian** setting? Why? _____

7. If you were an employer, would you rather hire someone who had **versatility** or someone who had **culpability**? Explain your answer. _____

Name: _____   Date: _____

Building Vocabulary Skills and Strategies, Level 7 • Saddleback Publishing, Inc. ©2004 • 3 Watson, Irvine, CA 92618 • Phone (888) SDL-BACK • www.sdlback.com   117

SHOPPING WORDS 1

Directions: Unscramble the words that match the definitions. Then use the unscrambled words to complete the crossword puzzle. Item 2-Across has been done for you.

ACROSS

2. _compare_ (MACEROP) what you do with prices

6. _____ (CINDOSUT) an amount taken off the usual price

9. _____ (GREDINTINES) what's listed on a food label

10. _____ (BALEL) a tag on the inside of clothing

11. _____ (CRAYTOF) place where things are manufactured

12. _____ (PASOCRONIM) a smart kind of shopping

13. _____ (LESA) a special event in a store

14. _____ (TICERD) one way to pay for things

16. _____ (HAXENCEG) what to do if something doesn't fit

17. _____ (SMECICOTS) the department in a store where you buy lipsticks

18. _____ (EAGRUNATE) a warranty

DOWN

1. _____ (YALQUIT) what you look for in clothing

3. _____ (GACITPER) where you look for the cost of an item

4. _____ (RYD NEALC) an instruction for cleaning clothes (2 words)

5. _____ (THIGWLEGITH) feature you'd want in summer clothing

7. _____ (TEDPTARMNE) a section in a store

8. _____ (CEPRI) the cost to the customer

10. _____ (EGELIRNI) the department where you'd buy a nightgown

15. _____ (GERLA) the size for a big person

Name: _____ Date: _____

118 *Building Vocabulary Skills and Strategies, Level 7* • Saddleback Publishing, Inc. ©2004 • 3 Watson, Irvine, CA 92618 • Phone (888) SDL-BACK • www.sdlback.com

SHOPPING WORDS 2

Directions: Use the crossword puzzle answers to correctly complete the sentences.

1. Be sure to buy all the _____ you need to make a special meal; make sure you get everything you need.

2. Mabel buys all her clothing at the _____ outlet stores.

3. So the _____ won't show through, you might have to cut it out of a sheer shirt.

4. This _____ store sells clothing, household goods, cosmetics, and shoes.

5. It can be expensive to take care of clothes whose care instructions say, "_____ only."

6. You can often get a _____ on clothing that is out of season.

7. Doris gave her friend a gift receipt so she could _____ the gift if she didn't like it.

8. Clothing that is of poor _____ never lasts very long.

9. Patrick bought his mom some perfume at the _____ counter.

10. If you shop with a _____ card, you don't have to carry a lot of cash with you.

11. The _____ showed that the _____ had been marked down three times.

12. James bought his athletic shoes on _____ for 25 percent off.

Name: _____ **Date:** _____

Building Vocabulary Skills and Strategies, Level 7 • Saddleback Publishing, Inc. ©2004 • 3 Watson, Irvine, CA 92618 • Phone (888) SDL-BACK • www.sdlback.com   119

LAW WORDS 1

Directions: Unscramble the words that match the definitions. Then use the unscrambled words to complete the crossword puzzle. Item 2-Across has been done for you.

ACROSS

2. __swear__ (RESAW) — what you do when you take an oath
6. _____ (RYJU) — the people who decide guilt or innocence
7. _____ (STIFYET) — what witnesses do on the stand
9. _____ (RALPOE) — to release a prisoner early under certain conditions
10. _____ (ENECSTEN) — what the judge determines
11. _____ (LATIR) — the process of hearing a case in court
14. _____ (MASTIUMON) — a lawyer's closing argument
15. _____ (TANDFEEDN) — person accused of a crime
16. _____ (HTURT) — what witnesses are required to tell
17. _____ (GAURE) — what lawyers do in court
18. _____ (FEEDENS) — the team that protects the accused

DOWN

1. _____ (TINPILFAF) — another name for the accuser
3. _____ (SETWINS) — a person called to testify
4. _____ (ONIBATRPO) — a possible sentence for a minor first-time offense
5. _____ (ISOCRETPUNO) — the legal team that makes the accusation
6. _____ (TECJUIS) — what the legal system strives to achieve
8. _____ (DIRVECT) — what the jury arrives at in the jury room
12. _____ (TAOTRENY) — another word for lawyer
13. _____ (DEJUG) — person in charge in the courtroom

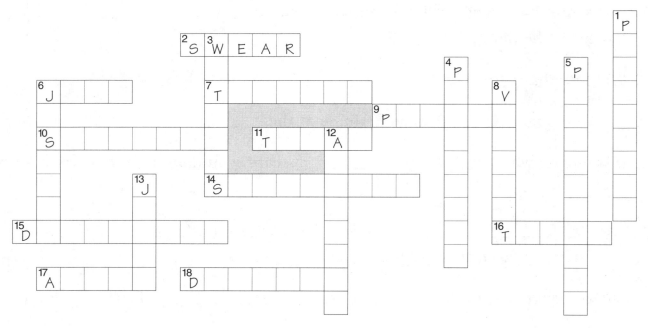

LAW WORDS 2

Directions: Use the crossword puzzle answers to correctly complete the sentences. You will use one word twice.

1. Every _____ must take an oath before taking the stand.

2. The teenager got six months' _____ for his minor offense.

3. The _____ of innocence was quite a surprise to everyone in the courtroom.

4. Every accused person is entitled to a fair _____.

5. A _____ of one's peers listens to the arguments made in court.

6. The lawyer for the _____ accused the young woman of stealing.

7. The newspaper reports showed sympathy for the _____, who had never been accused of anything before.

8. The _____ attorney claimed that his client had an airtight alibi.

9. The _____ called in a series of expert witnesses to back up the plaintiff's claim.

10. The witness had to swear to tell the _____.

11. The _____ wore a black robe and a serious expression.

12. The upset family of the convicted man said that _____ had not been served.

Name: _____   **Date:** _____

Building Vocabulary Skills and Strategies, Level 7 • Saddleback Publishing, Inc. ©2004 • 3 Watson, Irvine, CA 92618 • Phone (888) SDL-BACK • www.sdlback.com   121

BUILDING WORDS 1

Directions: Unscramble the words that match the definitions. Then use the unscrambled words to complete the crossword puzzle. Item 1-Across has been done for you.

ACROSS

1. _permits_ (PITREMS) — licenses the city issues to approve building plans
5. _____ (DAGSLIPNACN) — vegetation on the grounds around a building
6. _____ (ORNIGARITI) — system installed to carry water to plants
10. _____ (LOREBULDZ) — a piece of heavy equipment that moves dirt
11. _____ (TINUCTROSCON) — another word for the act of building
12. _____ (YADWLRL) — what covers a wall's framework on the inside
14. _____ (UTIFADONON) — the basis of any building
15. _____ (CHATTERIC) — the person who draws up plans for a building

DOWN

2. _____ (NIGSLEHS) — possible covering for a roof
3. _____ (TOPIA) — a concrete area, usually in the backyard
4. _____ (CETERILICNA) — the worker who installs wiring
7. _____ (LRPEUMB) — the worker who installs pipes
8. _____ (CRECTONE) — a liquid material that gradually becomes very hard
9. _____ (NORCROCTAT) — an independent worker who agrees to do a job
13. _____ (LUBRENPIT) — the drawn plan for a building

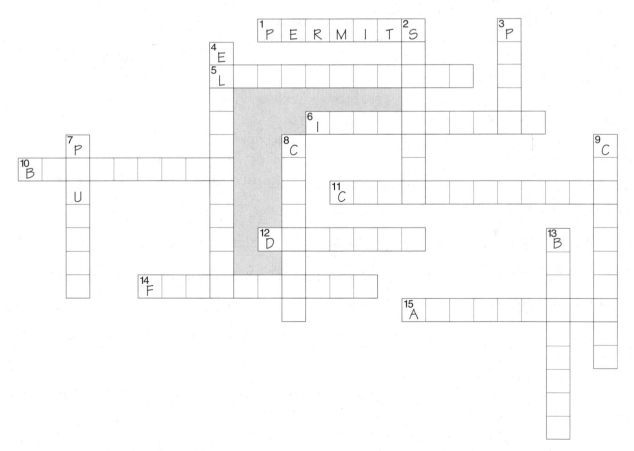

BUILDING WORDS 2

Directions: Use the crossword puzzle answers to correctly complete the sentences.

1. Once the basic _____ was in place, Helen added her favorite flowers here and there.

2. The _____ system in the yard consisted of 16 sprinklers and some drip hoses.

3. For the roof covering, George preferred _____ rather than tiles.

4. The general contractor referred to the _____ to see what the architect intended.

5. The _____ who drew up the plan is well-known in the city for his innovative designs.

6. The Johnsons enjoyed eating dinner on their new _____ in the backyard.

7. The _____ installed new pipes and fixtures in the bathroom and kitchen.

8. Because of zoning restrictions, the city was reluctant to issue _____ for an extra unit.

9. The _____ in the driveway had been stamped to look like cobblestones.

10. The _____ recommended installing lights under the kitchen cabinets.

11. _____ of the new home began in October and was completed in May.

12. The general _____ for the project hired people he had worked with before.

Name: _____   **Date:** _____

Building Vocabulary Skills and Strategies, Level 7 • Saddleback Publishing, Inc. ©2004 • 3 Watson, Irvine, CA 92618 • Phone (888) SDL-BACK • www.sdlback.com   123

SPACE WORDS 1

Directions: Unscramble the words that match the definitions. Then use the unscrambled words to complete the crossword puzzle. Item 2-Across has been done for you.

ACROSS

2. *propulsion* a force that causes forward movement
(PINPURSOLO)

6. _____ a jet-propelled device that shoots through the air
(CERTOK)

7. _____ between or among the stars
(TENLIRTALERS)

8. _____ a person who travels in space
(SORANTATU)

9. _____ the path taken by a celestial body or artificial satellite around its center of attraction
(BOIRT)

10. _____ to hurl or fling into space
(NUCLAH)

12. _____ something considered endless and without limits, such as space or time
(TINYINIF)

14. _____ the natural satellite of Earth
(ONMO)

16. _____ a celestial body that revolves around a larger celestial body
(LESALITTE)

17. _____ six types of particles thought to be basic units of matter
(RAQUKS)

DOWN

1. _____ a vehicle, such as a rocket or artificial satellite, designed for travel in outer space
(SCRTPEFACA)

3. _____ between or among planets
(RPIYRNATTENELA)

4. _____ a large system of celestial bodies
(LAYGAX)

5. _____ a force that draws bodies in the earth's sphere toward the center of the earth
(VIGATRY)

11. _____ the universe as a complete and harmonious system
(MOCOSS)

13. _____ any of the relatively large, non-glowing bodies that move in orbits around the sun
(PELTAN)

15. _____ a celestial body that sends pulses of radio waves at rapid, regular intervals
(LAPRUS)

Name: _____

Date: _____

124 *Building Vocabulary Skills and Strategies, Level 7* • Saddleback Publishing, Inc. ©2004 • 3 Watson, Irvine, CA 92618 • Phone (888) SDL-BACK • www.sdlback.com

SPACE WORDS 2

Directions: Use the crossword puzzle answers to correctly complete the sentences.

1. Sally Ride was the first female American _____ to go into space.

2. A _____ is used to propel fireworks, missiles, and space vehicles.

3. NASA plans to _____ another rocket in about three months.

4. The weather satellite is now in _____ around Earth.

5. Once a spaceship enters the atmosphere, the force of _____ pulls it toward Earth.

6. Earth is part of a _____ called the Milky Way.

7. Jupiter is the largest _____ in our solar system.

8. Our _____ revolves around the earth but does not rotate on an axis.

9. Because of the great distances between stars, _____ travel would take light years.

10. _____ travel seems within the reach of science in the relatively near future.

11. Scientists record the radio waves sent by the distant _____.

12. No scientist has ever actually seen a _____.

Name: _____   **Date:** _____

Building Vocabulary Skills and Strategies, Level 7 • Saddleback Publishing, Inc. ©2004 • 3 Watson, Irvine, CA 92618 • Phone (888) SDL-BACK • www.sdlback.com   125

HEALTH WORDS 1

Directions: Unscramble the words that match the definitions. Then use the unscrambled words to complete the crossword puzzle. Item 4-Across has been done for you.

ACROSS

4. _muscular_ (SMUURLAC) This type of person is very strong.

6. _____ (STESRS) emotional or mental strain or tension

9. _____ (NITAVMI) an organic substance found in most natural foods and needed for good health

10. _____ (PILCRALAY) any of the narrow, threadlike blood vessels connecting arteries with veins

13. _____ (BEFRI) coarse food parts that stimulate the movement of food through the intestines

14. _____ (PILDI) any of a group of organic compounds including fats, oils, and waxes

15. _____ (MANTERTET) what you need if you get sick

16. _____ (BEHRAETAT) what a doctor listens for with a stethoscope

DOWN

1. _____ (LACIVCADSROAUR) relating to the health of your heart and blood vessels

2. _____ (NORNIUITT) food; nourishment

3. _____ (SNIMIONA) difficulty in sleeping; sleeplessness

4. _____ (NELIRMA) a natural substance necessary to the human diet

5. _____ (DATCYAHROBRES) starches such as rice, potatoes, pasta, bread

7. _____ (TUAGFIE) a weary condition resulting from hard work, effort, or strain

8. _____ (TIMELOMABS) the rate at which your body burns calories

11. _____ (TCSERTH) what you need to do before exercising to avoid injury

12. _____ (MOSTYPM) a sign of an illness

126 *Building Vocabulary Skills and Strategies, Level 7* • Saddleback Publishing, Inc. ©2004 • 3 Watson, Irvine, CA 92618 • Phone (888) SDL-BACK • www.sdlback.com

HEALTH WORDS 2

Directions: Use the crossword puzzle answers to correctly complete the sentences.

1. Gene takes a _____
   pill the first thing each morning.

2. Foods that are good for quick
   energy before a race are
   _____.

3. Because she works out
   regularly, Gretchen has a very
   _____ body.

4. Good _____,
   proper rest, and adequate exercise
   are necessary for good health.

5. Before and after his workouts, Timothy
   likes to slowly _____ his muscles.

6. During aerobic exercise, you should raise your _____
   for at least 20 minutes.

7. Edward is under a great deal of _____ at work, which is
   making him ill.

8. One way to build strong muscles is to work them to _____
   and then rest.

9. You might be able to cure _____ by getting plenty of
   exercise during the day.

10. The first _____ of a cold might be a scratchy throat.

11. The more muscular you are, the higher your rate of _____
    will be.

12. The best _____ for a cold is rest and plenty of liquids.

Name: _____   **Date:** _____

Building Vocabulary Skills and Strategies, Level 7 • Saddleback Publishing, Inc. ©2004 • 3 Watson, Irvine, CA 92618 • Phone (888) SDL-BACK • www.sdlback.com   127

BUSINESS WORDS 1

Directions: Unscramble the words that match the definitions. Then use the unscrambled words to complete the crossword puzzle. Item 1-Across has been done for you.

ACROSS

1. _cubicle_ a small work enclosure
   (ECICBUL)
4. _____ one who helps another
   (SIATSANST)
7. _____ a customer
   (LECTIN)
8. _____ a paid worker
   (EPEYMOLE)
12. _____ one who writes letters and performs other administrative duties
    (RESARCETY)
13. _____ work beyond 40 hours
    (MEROTIVE)
14. _____ the date something is due
    (EDILEDAN)
15. _____ a gathering
    (MINETEG)

DOWN

2. _____ things employees get in addition to their regular pay, such as insurance, vacation pay, sick pay
   (FEBIENTS)
3. _____ one who hires others
   (MYRELOPE)
5. _____ a worker's pay
   (ASRAYL)
6. _____ a group of people working together
   (MITECOTME)
7. _____ a meeting at which a discussion is held
   (FENECEORNC)
9. _____ time off from work
   (NOCAVIAT)
10. _____ the head of a company
    (SIPERNTED)
11. _____ an assignment
    (JCTPORE)

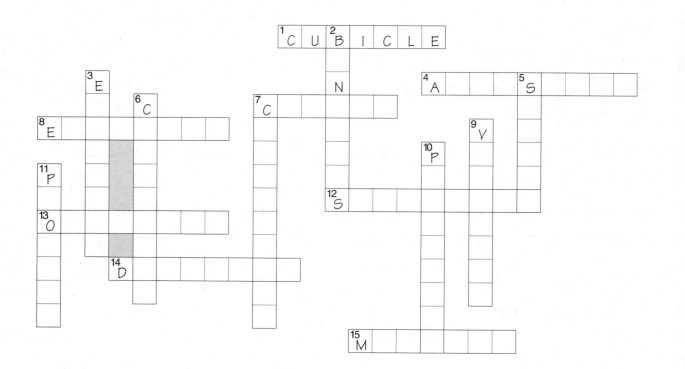

BUSINESS WORDS 2

Directions: Use the crossword puzzle answers to correctly complete the sentences.

1. When he took his _____,
   Brad went fly-fishing in Montana.

2. The _____
   requested that his parts be
   manufactured in three months.

3. Mark, Joel, Katie, and Julia are
   on the _____
   to plan the company picnic.

4. As an _____
   of this company, you are expected
   to get to work by nine o'clock.

5. This is a huge _____,
   and we'll need everyone's cooperation to finish it.

6. The _____ for the new project is July 18.

7. The ad claimed, "We are an equal-opportunity _____."

8. The _____ at this company include a yearly two-week
   paid vacation and 10 paid sick days.

9. Diane's _____ was 10 percent higher than it had
   been at her previous job.

10. Pete gets paid time-and-a-half for working _____.

11. As Alicia's _____, Tyrone is responsible for all of her
    clerical work.

12. Jacob is the _____ and chief executive officer of
    his own company.

Name: _____   **Date:** _____

Building Vocabulary Skills and Strategies, Level 7 • Saddleback Publishing, Inc. ©2004 • 3 Watson, Irvine, CA 92618 • Phone (888) SDL-BACK • www.sdlback.com   129

TRAVEL WORDS 1

Directions: Unscramble the words that match the definitions. Then use the unscrambled words to complete the crossword puzzle. Item 1-Across has been done for you.

ACROSS

1. *tropical* the climate in Hawaii
   (PORTCLAI)

3. _____ a popular tourist activity in Africa
   (ISARAF)

4. _____ the type of identification you need to travel internationally
   (SAPOPRST)

7. _____ a place to eat when you're on vacation
   (TENRURASAT)

9. _____ lodgings; room and board
   (OMAMTIDACOONCS)

12. _____ a place to sleep when you're on vacation
   (THEOL)

13. _____ the kind of trips tourists often like to take
   (IGNIGSTHESE)

15. _____ a popular tourist attraction in Egypt
   (DRAPMIYS)

16. _____ what a tourist likes to buy
   (VUISEONR)

17. _____ what you must do to understand a foreign language
   (LATANRSET)

DOWN

2. _____ what it costs to fly on a plane
   (FARRIAE)

3. _____ what you carry your clothes in
   (CUASIETS)

5. _____ planes, trains, and taxis, for example
   (TISNAPTROTRANO)

6. _____ a checkpoint where luggage is examined for safety
   (TYCUSREI)

8. _____ what tourists like to take with cameras
   (HHOTPAGORPS)

10. _____ a place to see a country's artworks
   (UMSEMU)

11. _____ a person who might take you around, pointing out the sights
   (UDGIE)

14. _____ a person who visits another city or country
   (TOITRUS)

130 *Building Vocabulary Skills and Strategies, Level 7* • Saddleback Publishing, Inc. ©2004 • 3 Watson, Irvine, CA 92618 • Phone (888) SDL-BACK • www.sdlback.com

TRAVEL WORDS 2

Directions: Use the crossword puzzle answers to correctly complete the sentences.

1. The _____ are the ancient burial places of Egyptian pharaohs.

2. While on vacation Jenny's favorite means of _____ is a bicycle.

3. Mona's _____ picture is unusually good.

4. At the _____ checkpoint, Martha had to take off her shoes and her jacket.

5. The _____ on that airline includes a meal and a movie.

6. Jed had to buy a bigger _____ so he could pack enough clothes for his trip.

7. Marianne's _____ room was a large one overlooking Central Park.

8. Ted's _____ plans included a visit to the Lincoln Memorial.

9. Victoria speaks French, so she can _____ for Dan when they're in Paris.

10. The only _____ Hank bought in Mexico was a sombrero.

11. Cynthia took more than 200 _____, some in color and some in black and white.

12. On her African _____, Karen saw zebras, elephants, and lions.

Name: _____   Date: _____

Building Vocabulary Skills and Strategies, Level 7 • Saddleback Publishing, Inc. ©2004 • 3 Watson, Irvine, CA 92618 • Phone (888) SDL-BACK • www.sdlback.com   131

GOVERNMENT WORDS 1

Directions: Unscramble the words that match the definitions. Then use the unscrambled words to complete the crossword puzzle. Item 4-Across has been done for you.

ACROSS

4. _executive_ (ECEUTXIEV) — having the duty and power of putting laws into effect

6. _____ (REPBAMEL) — the introductory section of the Constitution

7. _____ (DANENSMEMT) — changes and additions to the Constitution

9. _____ (UCLJIADI) — the branch of government of which the courts are a part

11. _____ (TAMECDOR) — a member of one of the major political parties in the U.S.

13. _____ (VELSIELAGTI) — the branch of government responsible for passing laws

14. _____ (PIAMCEH) — to formally charge a public official with wrongdoing in office

15. _____ (GYANEC) — a governmental bureau that carries out a certain kind business

16. _____ (BAETCIN) — a group of official advisers and assistants to the president

DOWN

1. _____ (BYLTOSBI) — a person who tries to influence legislators in favor of some special interest

2. _____ (CETOLREAL) — having to do with an election or electors

3. _____ (PLIRBCEUAN) — a member of one of the major political parties in the U.S.

5. _____ (TTICOOINUSTN) — the fundamental body of laws governing the U.S.

8. _____ (ESTNEA) — the upper house of the U.S. Congress

10. _____ (NOESDICI) — a conclusion or judgment made by the Supreme Court

12. _____ (CETLE) — to choose by voting

132 _Building Vocabulary Skills and Strategies, Level 7_ • Saddleback Publishing, Inc. ©2004 • 3 Watson, Irvine, CA 92618 • Phone (888) SDL-BACK • www.sdlback.com

GOVERNMENT WORDS 2

Directions: Use the crossword puzzle answers to correctly complete the sentences.

1. The _____ of the United States consists of seven articles.

2. Some 26 _____ have been made to the Constitution.

3. The Supreme Court is the highest body in the _____ branch.

4. The _____ office in the United States is held by the president.

5. Congress makes up the _____ branch of the federal government.

6. The _____ has 100 members, two from each state.

7. John F. Kennedy was a _____.

8. Ronald Reagan was a _____.

9. The _____ to the Constitution begins with the words "We the people of the United States."

10. Members of the _____ give the president information and advice.

11. The president is elected by members of the _____ college.

12. A _____ uses many methods to influence legislators on behalf of special interests.

13. The Supreme Court's job is to make _____ about important legal cases.

Name: _____   Date: _____

Building Vocabulary Skills and Strategies, Level 7 • Saddleback Publishing, Inc. ©2004 • 3 Watson, Irvine, CA 92618 • Phone (888) SDL-BACK • www.sdlback.com   133

PARTY WORDS 1

Directions: Unscramble the words that match the definitions. Then use the unscrambled words to complete the crossword puzzle. Item 2-Across has been done for you.

ACROSS

2. _occasion_ (SOCANOCI) — a special reason for a party
7. _____ (SGSUTE) — people who come to a party
8. _____ (LAGA) — a lively celebration
10. _____ (STFEMREERSHN) — food and drink served at a party
13. _____ (TNERETANINTEM) — what a band provides at a party
14. _____ (TRUNINODICOT) — how to acquaint two strangers with each other
15. _____ (TONITIRNEAC) — how people relate to each other at a party
16. _____ (MASEMEUNT) — the condition of being happy or diverted

DOWN

1. _____ (NATCOVSERINO) — friendly, informal talk between persons
3. _____ (RETCARE) — a person who makes and serves food for a party
4. _____ (RENPRAT) — the one with whom you dance
5. _____ (BETCREILANO) — recognition of a special event with a party
6. _____ (QUBAENT) — an elaborate meal or feast
9. _____ (RESAZPEPIT) — food served before the main course
11. _____ (NETEV) — an important happening
12. _____ (RAFLOM) — requiring elaborate dress and manners

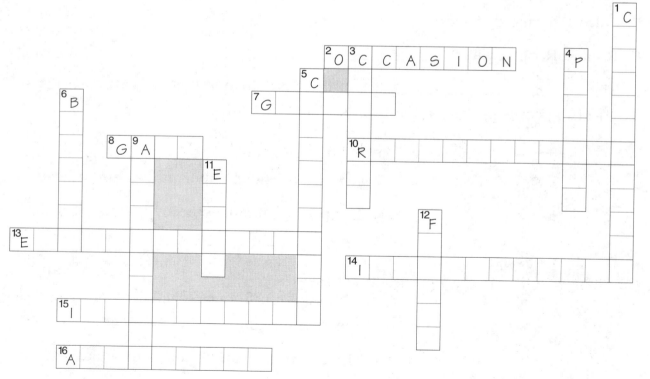

PARTY WORDS 2

Directions: Use the crossword puzzle answers to correctly complete the sentences.

1. _____ at the afternoon party included appetizers and beverages.

2. _____ dress was required, so Richard rented a tuxedo.

3. A good _____ should provide each person with some information about the other.

4. As the party ended, Meg and Dylan were in the middle of a long _____.

5. Michelle's dance _____ knows all the latest steps.

6. The _____ for the party was Jeffrey's sixteenth birthday.

7. All of the _____ had a wonderful time at the party.

8. The _____ of Arielle's graduation lasted for three days.

9. The band, the singer, and the clown all provided _____ for the party guests.

10. The _____ table was adorned with fine linen and sparkling crystal.

11. About an hour before the main course, the _____ were served.

12. The food prepared by the young _____ was quite delicious.

Name: _____   Date: _____

SCOPE & SEQUENCE

STUDENT	FORMAL/INFORMAL LANGUAGE	DICTIONARY ENTRIES	DENOTATION	CONNOTATION	EUPHEMISMS/DYSPHEMISMS	PRONUNCIATION	SILENT LETTERS	SYLLABICATION	ACCENT MARKS	CONTEXT CLUES	VARIANT WORD FORMS	COMPOUND WORDS	GREEK ROOTS	LATIN ROOTS	PREFIXES	SUFFIXES	NEAR MISSES	SYNONYMS: NOUNS	SYNONYMS: VERBS	SYNONYMS: ADJECTIVES

SCOPE & SEQUENCE

STUDENT	SYNONYMS: ADVERBS	ANTONYMS: NOUNS	ANTONYMS: VERBS	ANTONYMS: ADJECTIVES	ANTONYMS: ADVERBS	HOMOPHONES	HOMOGRAPHS	CLIPPED WORDS	FOREIGN WORDS	INTERPRETING IDIOMS	EXPLORING BIG WORDS	SHOPPING WORDS	LAW WORDS	BUILDING WORDS	SPACE WORDS	HEALTH WORDS	BUSINESS WORDS	TRAVEL WORDS	GOVERNMENT WORDS	PARTY WORDS

Building Vocabulary Skills and Strategies, Level 7 • Saddleback Publishing, Inc. ©2004 • 3 Watson, Irvine, CA 92618 • Phone (888) SDL-BACK • www.sdlback.com

ANSWER KEY

PAGE 6
A. 1. perceive
2. calculate
3. abolish
4. signify
5. perturb
6. massive
7. baffle
8. notable
9. tedious
10. quest
B. 1. b 3. a 5. c
2. c 4. a

PAGE 7
A. 1. handle
2. bugs
3. ditzy
4. chill
5. sleazy
6. hangout
7. batty
B. 1. melancholy
2. cheap
3. observe
4. refined
5. gab
6. dis

PAGE 8
A. 1. mentor   3. first
2. third   4. erudite
B. 1. adjourn
2. ballast
3. cyclone
4. demerit
5. erupt
6. fragile
7. genial
8. geology
9. heifer
10. inquiry
11. jazz
12. kidnap
13. lapel
14. lavish
15. matrimony
16. oblong
17. romance
18. sentiment
19. wary
20. yonder
21. zenith

PAGE 9
A. 1. The following words
should be crossed out:
mayfly, material, maze.
2. Answers will vary but
might include
mathematics, matriarch,
matter, and matrix.
B. 1. between   3. will
2. forward   4. before
C. The following words should
be circled: geezer, general,
gelatin; plowshare, ploy,
plummet, plow.

PAGE 10
A. 1. agonies
2. tomatoes
3. fathers-in-law
4. mice
5. thieves
6. radii
B. 1. write   3. gone
2. fed   4. sit
C. 1. most attractive
2. more bored
3. fewest
4. more colossal

PAGE 11
A. 1. omelet
2. octopi
3. larvae
4. tepee
5. levelled
6. gladioli
7. makeup
8. halleluiah
B. 1. e   3. d   5. f   7. c
2. b   4. g   6. a

PAGE 12
A. 1. N   4. N   7. P   10. N
2. P   5. P   8. N   11. P
3. P   6. N   9. P   12. N
B. 1. devise
2. assertive
3. crowd
4. accumulate
5. persuade
6. bold
7. custodian
8. aroma
9. emphasize
10. thin

PAGE 13
1. pig-headed
2. emotional
3. donation
4. abandon
5. help
6. special
7. third-world country
8. disabled
9. employee
10. soldier
11. cur
12. mansion
13. restroom

PAGE 14
Approximate answers:
1. *Redolent* because a
pelargonium is a flower, and
redolent refers to smell.
2. Qishm: Iran; Qiqihar: China
3. *Mellifluous* because the word
means "melodious," whereas
cacophonous means "harsh-
sounding."
4. No; a *boutique* sells clothing,
accessories, and gifts. *Borscht*
is cold beet soup.

5. *Progenitors* because the words
describe ancestors. *Progeny*
refers to descendants.
6. An *epicure* because he or she
appreciates fine food, whereas
a *gourmand* will eat anything
without discrimination.
7. *Ameliorate* because the word
means "to improve";
exacerbate means "to make
worse."

PAGE 15
Approximate answers:
1. No; a *eulogy* is a funeral
oration, and a *euglena* is a
microscopic organism.
2. They are all open land areas.
3. Greece
4. A *coati* is a small tree-
dwelling, raccoonlike
carnivore with a long flexible
snout, found in Mexico and
Central and South America.
An *agouti* is a rabbit-sized
nocturnal rodent with grizzled
fur, found in tropical America.
What they have in common is
that they are both small land
animals found in the Western
Hemisphere. One difference is
that the coati lives in trees,
and the agouti does not.
5. *Amiable,* because an amiable
child is friendly and pleasant,
whereas an *obstreperous* one
is disobedient and
unpleasant.
6. You might give an
octogenarian (a person in his
or her eighties) a *cymbidium*
(an orchid) on his or her
birthday, Mother's Day,
Father's Day, or any other
special occasion.
7. No, because a *tyro* is a
beginner and a *virtuoso* is
an expert.

PAGE 16
A SOUNDS
1. back, began
2. basic, volcano
3. almost, falter
4. beware, square
5. hard, party
6. another, agree
E SOUNDS
1. empty, spell
2. secret, female
3. something, operate, safety
4. baker, camera
5. happen, item, weapon
I SOUNDS
1. insect, which
2. wire, describe
3. dirty, shirt

O SOUNDS
1. opera, problem
2. ocean, cargo
3. sound, eyebrow
4. voice, joyous
5. song, office
6. cookie, wooden
7. troop, bamboo
8. canyon, method

PAGE 17
A. U SOUNDS
1. funny, summer
2. January, human
3. bullfrog, cushion
4. prune, cruel
5. turtle, surface
B. 1. there   6. pillow
2. pie   7. sauerkraut
3. flown   8. hood
4. treasure   9. plowed
5. plead   10. enough

PAGE 18
A.
	SILENT LETTER	CROSS OUT
1.	c	inspect, color
2.	h	showing, happy
3.	w	wander, wilt
4.	t	water, patted
5.	l	flap, tassel
6.	g	gather, sugar
7.	b	buzz, amber
8.	k	broken, mark
9.	p	perhaps, important

B. 1. black   4. two, four, five,
2. heart   eight, nine
3. science 5. descend

PAGE 19
A. 1. buffet   4. mistletoe
2. croquet   5. wretched
3. khaki   6. adjoining
B. ACROSS: 1. sight 4. honest
5. batch 9. debtor
DOWN: 2. thigh 3. reign
5. bristle 6. cartridge
7. lacquer 8. midget

PAGE 20
A. 1. **2-SYLLABLE WORDS**
block • ade
tal • low
or • chid
2. **3-SYLLABLE WORDS**
ac • knowl • edge
bun • ga • low
o • ver • sight
com • e • dy
3. **4-SYLLABLE WORDS**
con • tin • u • ous
mel • an • chol • y
af • fec • tion • ate
con • sid • er • ate
4. **5-SYLLABLE WORDS**
dis • a • gree • a • ble
ge • o • log • i • cal
de • vel • op • men • tal
or • gan • i • za • tion

138

PAGE 20 (continued)
B. 1. ATlas
2. phenOMenon
3. COMplicate
4. irREGular

PAGE 21
A. 1. first   5. second
2. first   6. third
3. first   7. second
4. third   8. second
B. 1. contest (noun): accent
first syllable
contest (verb): accent
second syllable
2. conduct (verb): accent
second syllable
conduct (noun): accent
first syllable
3. replay (noun): accent
first syllable
replay (verb): accent
second syllable
4. address (verb): accent
second syllable
address (noun): accent
first syllable

PAGE 22
1. jimple: a
2. dipdop: c
3. krinskis: b
4. sloozed: a
5. schlimper: b
6. gairblue: c
7. flang: a
8. moglump: c

PAGE 23
1. a 2. b 3. c 4. c 5. a 6. c

PAGE 24
1. impulse   5. film
2. honesty   6. attempt
3. players   7. rainfall
4. search   8. position

PAGE 25
1. operate   6. injured
2. forces   7. perform
3. complain   8. fainted
4. contrasted   9. tempt
5. conquered   10. scorch

PAGE 26
1. peaceful   6. difficult
2. destitute   7. firm
3. speechless   8. simple
4. bashful   9. humble
5. hectic   10. leisurely

PAGE 27
1. approximately
2. reluctantly
3. thoroughly
4. cordially
5. formerly
6. fundamentally
7. partially
8. violently
9. never
10. continuously

PAGE 28
A. ACROSS: 4. creation
5. brutality   6. gland
7. solitude
DOWN: 1. accuracy
2. hostility   3. prestige
4. change
B. 1. gland   5. prestige
2. change   6. brutality
3. creation   7. hostility
4. solitude   8. accuracy

PAGE 29
Sentences will vary; check for
correct use of the nouns.
1. affection
2. consideration
3. eternity
4. fearlessness
5. venom
6. turbulence
7. suspicion
8. sentiment
9. resident
10. punctuality
11. monotony

PAGE 30
A. ACROSS: 2. preferable
4. filtered   6. punctuated
8. dried
DOWN: 1. warranted
3. dimpled   5. dead
7. tied
B. 1. dead
2. preferable
3. dimpled
4. filtered
5. dried
6. punctuated
C. Sentences will vary; check
for correct use of the
adjectives.
1. believable
2. enjoyable
3. preferable

PAGE 31
Sentences will vary; check for
correct use of the adjectives.
1. sustained or sustainable
2. warped
3. rejected
4. radiant
5. rebellious
6. recognizable
7. excellent
8. successful
9. modified
10. persistent
11. intentional or intended

PAGE 32
A. ACROSS: 3. consume   4. drape
5. rescue   6. hate
DOWN: 1. dramatize
2. depend   3. complicate

B. 1. rescue   5. depend
2. hate   6. complicate
3. consume   7. drape
4. dramatize

PAGE 33
Sentences will vary; check for
correct use of the verb.
1. postpone
2. lubricate
3. convict
4. confront
5. correspond
6. develop
7. organize
8. penetrate
9. paralyze
10. narrate
11. represent

PAGE 34
A. 2. bare, dare, hare
3. ride, side, hide
4. pest, test, best
5. beak, leak, teak
6. boot, root, loot
B. 1. track, stack, black
2. creep, sleep, cheep
3. chill, still, grill
4. brake, flake, drake

PAGE 35
A. 2. flash, flag, fact
3. brain, blob, bold
4. pale, pant, parch
5. cart, core, creek
6. none, nail, neither
B. 1. plant, fort, cart (or plane,
fore, care)
2. pang, tang, bang
3. form, norm, warm
4. tarp, seep, damp
C. Possible answers:
2. frame (or flame)
3. baste
4. bang
5. coat (or colt)
6. hung
7. posse (or prose)
8. line (or lice, like)

PAGE 36
A. 2. c, wristwatch
3. e, airport
4. i, outside
5. a, scarecrow
6. l, touchdown
7. d, waterfall
8. g, overbite
9. h, pancake
10. m, skyscraper
11. f, silverware
12. b, paperback
13. k, breakfast
B. Student art will vary.

PAGE 37
A. 1. tiptoe
2. cupboard
3. peppermint
4. spotlight
5. highchair
6. sweatshirt
7. windmill
B. ACROSS: 1. flashback
4. outfit   6. pigtail
7. dishpan
DOWN: 2. lifeguard
3. carpool   5. goldfish
6. postcard

PAGE 38
A. 1. headphone, d
2. footbridge, e
3. footnote, f
4. headlights or footlights, g
5. footprint, a
6. footstool, c
7. headline, b
B. ACROSS: 2. headhunter
5. Football   6. headband
DOWN: 1. headache
3. headquarters
4. footboard   5. footlocker

PAGE 39
1. headdresses
2. foothold
3. headboard
4. headfirst
5. footwear
6. headset
7. footsteps
8. footloose
9. headway
10. footpath
11. footrace
12. headlock

PAGE 40
A. 1. airtight
2. waterlily
3. airmail
4. waterlogged
5. airport
6. waterfall
B. ACROSS: 2. airwaves
4. watercolors   5. airsick
6. watermelon   7. waterline
DOWN: 1. waterfront
3. airbrush

PAGE 41
1. waterfowl
2. watermark
3. airsafe or airworthy
4. waterproof or
water-repellent
5. airstrike
6. watercress
7. airborne
8. airplane
9. watertight
10. airspace
11. waterfall

139

PAGE 42

A. 1. windbag, d
2. sunglasses, f
3. windsock, g
4. sundown, a
5. sunrise, b
6. windbreaker, c
7. sundial, e

B. ACROSS: 1. windstorms
4. sunburn 6. windsurfed
7. sustan 8. windshield
DOWN: 2. sunbonnet
3. sunroof 5. windfall

PAGE 43

1. windjammer
2. sunbeam
3. windchill
4. windmills
5. sunlamp
6. windpipe
7. sunbathe
8. sunfish
9. windblown
10. sunscreen
11. sunflower

PAGE 44

A. Answers will vary. Possible
answers:

G or S	SAMPLE ANSWER
3. G	elephant
4. S	gem
5. G	bracelet
6. G	rose
7. S	color
8. S	fish

B. Answers can appear in any
order.

foolish—absurd;
hobby—obsession;
glad—ecstatic;
entertain—enthrall;
apologize—atone;
influence—domination;
admire—adore;
disagree—oppose;
alone—isolated

PAGE 45

Sentences will vary; check for
correct use of the words.

SCRAMBLED WORDS:
2. amuse 5. sprint
3. engaging 6. glum
4. respond

PAGE 46

1. prognosis
2. telegram
3. cardiologist
4. tricycle
5. symphony
6. paleolithic
7. epidemic
8. polyandry
9. microphone
10. phonics
11. cyclops
12. Democrat

PAGE 47

A. 1. d 3. e 5. a
2. c 4. f 6. b

B. 1. eye
2. fear of
3. god

C. Possible answers:
1. cinema
2. paralysis
3. maniac
4. anesthetist

PAGE 48

1. submarine
2. recognized
3. manuscript
4. cordial
5. recliner
6. pedestrians
7. donated
8. curable
9. marines
10. manufacturing
11. quadrupeds

PAGE 49

A. 1. move 4. faith
2. see 5. war
3. move 6. common

B. Possible answers:
1. altimeter
2. gratuitous
3. documentary
4. paternity

PAGE 50

1. prototype
2. polygamy
3. quintuplets
4. contraindicated
5. benefactor
6. comfort
7. extraordinary
8. octet
9. polynomial
10. benediction

PAGE 51

A. 1. self 4. million
2. not 5. around
3. false 6. small

B. 1. embraced 4. embroider
2. enclose 5. enchanted
3. embezzle 6. encourage

PAGE 52

1. vacancy
2. fortitude
3. childhood
4. racism
5. capitalization
6. honesty
7. pallor
8. bravery
9. standardization
10. pacifism
11. fervor

PAGE 53

A. 1. maternal
2. statuesque
3. circular
4. military
5. picturesque
6. popular
7. natural

B. 1. fearful
2. Turbulent
3. nervous
4. comatose
5. successful
6. glorious

PAGE 54

1. collision
2. expand
3. loose
4. adopt
5. pursue
6. personnel
7. finally
8. voracious
9. perpetuate
10. deprived
11. calendar

PAGE 55

A. ACROSS: 3. lose 5. perpetrate
7. peruse 8. collusion
DOWN: 1. colander
2. depraved 4. veracious
6. finely

B. 1. d
2. g
3. b
4. i
5. a
6. j
7. c
8. e
9. f
10. h

PAGE 56

2. e, cavity
3. a, dwelling
4. c, flattery
5. i, ban
6. d, exaggeration
7. h, glint
8. f, haste
9. g, hatred
10. j, instructor

PAGE 57

1. rucksack
2. magician
3. competitor
4. passion
5. siege
6. storm
7. vase
8. temptation
9. testimony

PAGE 58

A. 1. insult
2. assure
3. induce
4. waver
5. invalidate
6. admit
7. catch
8. toss
9. expel

B. 1. deserve, justify
2. choose, prefer
3. harass, victimize
4. untangle, untwist
5. burn, char
6. appraise, assess
7. handy, suitable
8. differ, digress
9. curve, bend

PAGE 59

A. 1. lead
2. examine
3. cover
4. punch
5. soil
6. surround

B. Possible answers:
1. nap
2. mark
3. stink
4. entice
5. affect

C. Sentences will vary.
Check for correct use
of the synonyms.

PAGE 60

1. d, genuine
2. g, aged
3. i, ambitious
4. a, irritated
5. e, flimsy
6. j, changeable
7. c, received
8. f, miniature
9. h, hardy
10. b, intellectual

PAGE 61

A. 1. fancy, showy
2. manly, male
3. loyal, dependable
4. dangerous, risky
5. unique, unusual
6. pictorial, scenic

B. Possible answers:
1. catching
2. female
3. tasty
4. rebellious
5. terrific
6. tiny

PAGE 62
A.
1. h 6. e
2. d 7. i
3. g 8. j
4. b 9. f
5. a 10. c

B. **ACROSS:** 3. gladly 6. surely
8. completely
DOWN: 1. seldom 2. clearly
4. honestly 5. eternally
7. roughly

PAGE 63
1. first, originally
2. totally, entirely
3. simply, utterly
4. blindly, mindlessly
5. very, quite
6. accidentally, mistakenly
7. extremely, greatly
8. unusually, remarkably

PAGE 64
A.
1. c 3. a 5. i 7. h
2. f 4. e 6. l 8. j
9. b 10. d 11. g 12. k

B.
1. vigor
2. toil
3. clarity
4. patriotism
5. evil
6. maturity
7. foreground
8. jollity

C. Sentences will vary; check
for correct use of the
antonyms.
1. unity
2. reason
3. gentleman
4. rashness

PAGE 65
A. Answers can be in any
order.
1. attic / cellar
2. brightness / dullness
3. cowardice / heroism
4. assistance / hindrance
5. fairness / injustice
6. deflation / inflation
7. courtesy / disrespect
8. elimination / inclusion
9. decision / hesitation
10. punishment / pardon
11. firmness / flabbiness
12. employed / jobless
13. triviality / importance
14. laughter / weeping

B. **ACROSS:** 2. escape 5. gainer
6. clarity 7. defend
DOWN: 1. roughness
3. poverty 4. knowledge

PAGE 66
1. abbreviate
2. disconnect
3. convicted
4. welcome
5. repel
6. ignored
7. released
8. improved
9. loosened

PAGE 67
A.
1. arrive
2. freeze
3. include
4. submit
5. envy
6. approach
7. sell
8. forbid
9. mock
10. conceal

B. **ACROSS:** 2. wrinkle 4. quarrel
7. finish 8. simplify
DOWN: 1. harden 3. excite
5. reveal 6. hire

PAGE 68
A.
1. formal
2. passive
3. straight
4. cherished
5. proud
6. imaginary
7. crowded
8. alien

B.
1. resistant
2. delicate
3. elongated
4. lowered
5. comfortable
6. bound
7. harmless
8. optimistic

PAGE 69
A.
1. gloomy
2. external
3. common
4. copied
5. brief
6. irrational
7. unruly
8. able
9. unethical
10. adequate

B. **ACROSS:** 4. inactive 6. lying
7. coarse
DOWN: 1. stingy 2. parched
3. refined 5. moral

PAGE 70
A.
1. abruptly
2. foolishly
3. often
4. brightly
5. briskly
6. certainly
7. unhappily
8. accidentally
9. thoughtfully

B. **ACROSS:** 3. carefully 5. fully
6. gently 7. crazily
DOWN: 1. clearly 2. listlessly
4. rudely 5. fairly

PAGE 71
A. Pairs of adverbs can be in
any order.
2. definitely, questionably
3. commonly, unusually
4. obscurely, famously
5. awkwardly, gracefully
6. sometimes, invariably

B. **ACROSS:** 1. unluckily
6. sourly 7. safely
8. invariably 9. slowly
DOWN: 2. cruelly
3. unclearly 4. commonly
5. passively

PAGE 72
A.
1. aloud 7. scent
2. cruise 8. mane
3. lye 9. won
4. bawl
5. fined
6. meat or mete

B. **ACROSS:** 2. complement
4. hymn 5. whose
7. moan 8. pore 9. chute
10. aweigh
DOWN: 1. holy 3. tee
5. weave 6. shown
8. pause

C. 1. (circle buoy, fur, and
beach) The boy climbed
up the fir tree and the
beech tree.
2. (circle wee, fore, and
flairs) After the accident,
we set off four flares to
get attention.

PAGE 73
A. 1. barred bard
2. barque bark
3. boll bowl
4. serial cereal
5. kernels for colonels
6. night knight
7. high hi

B. 1. fryer friar
2. hostile hostel
3. plait plate
4. prophet for profit
5. pale pail
6. seen scene

PAGE 74
A.
2. pine
3. compound
4. blow
5. fine
6. hide

B. Answer: *origins*
2. jar
3. pitcher
4. page
5. kind
6. down
7. fresh

PAGE 75
A. 1. bow: possible answer: a
knot with loops in it
2. blue: the color of the sky
3. corps: a large military
unit
4. hey: a cry used to attract
attention
5. lessen: to minimalize

B. 2–3. Answers will vary.
Check students' sentences
for correct use of the
homographs.

PAGE 76
A. 1. automobile
2. coeducational student
3. trigonometry
4. delicatessen
5. centum
6. cucumber
7. submarine
8. periwig

B. 1. vet
2. typo
3. lunch
4. deb
5. doc
6. mod
7. pants
8. mums

PAGE 77
A. **ACROSS:** 3. coattails
4. scramble 5. distillery
6. spectacles 7. percolate
DOWN: 1. lubricate 2. gabble

B. 1. hackney
2. curiosity
3. moving picture
4. penitentiary
5. turnpike
6. university
7. promenade

141

PAGE 78
A. 1. a 3. h 5. d 7. g
2. c 4. f 6. e 8. b
B. 1. named after Attabiya, a quarter in Baghdad
2. after Jean Martinet, a 17th century French army officer
3. after Rudolf Diesel, born in Paris of German parents, who improved the internal combustion engine
4. after John Duns Scotus, whose once accepted writings were ridiculed in the 16th century
5. after Joseph Guillotin, the 19th century French physician who invented it

PAGE 79
ACROSS: 3. bloomers 5. atlas
6. bowler 11. pasteurize
12. Friday
DOWN: 1. July
2. graham crackers
4. maverick 7. teddy bear
8. volt 9. jersey 10. May

PAGE 80
1. c 3. b 5. a 7. c
2. a 4. b 6. b

PAGE 81
1. a 4. j 7. d 10. e
2. g 5. i 8. b 11. k
3. h 6. f 9. c

PAGE 82
A. 1. a 3. b
2. c 4. a
B. 1. b 3. d 5. a 7. h
2. g 4. f 6. c 8. e

PAGE 83
1. carried on
2. drew a blank
3. dress down
4. looked up to
5. lost face
6. cut back
7. see eye to eye
8. take on
9. get ahead
10. kept at

PAGE 84
1. b 3. c 5. c 7. b
2. a 4. a 6. a 8. c

PAGE 85
1. c 3. b 5. a 7. a
2. a 4. b 6. c 8. b

PAGE 86
1. b 3. a 5. c 7. a
2. c 4. a 6. b 8. b

PAGE 87
A. 1. chickens
2. feet
3. heels
4. hoop
5. brains
B. 1. b 3. d 5. c
2. a 4. e

PAGE 88
1. b 3. b 5. c 7. a
2. c 4. a 6. a 8. b

PAGE 89
1. hold a candle to, playing second fiddle
2. eating them out of house and home, lay down the law
3. take it easy, make ends meet
4. come clean, turned a deaf ear to
5. make up for, pull strings
6. hit the nail on the head, fall short
7. have it both ways, get away with

PAGE 90
1. aerobics
2. belated
3. barge
4. barnacles
5. brocade
6. ability
7. accelerate
8. absorb
9. accessory
10. adhere
11. buoyant
12. agenda

PAGE 91
Answers will vary. Check students' sentences for correct use of the words.

PAGE 92
1. disguise
2. civilian
3. carbonated
4. dubious
5. cabaret
6. dahlia
7. credence
8. defiance
9. depreciate
10. custody
11. dexterity
12. cognizant

PAGE 93
Answers will vary. Check students' sentences for correct use of the words.

PAGE 94
1. escapade
2. flaunt
3. earnest
4. exceed
5. firmament
6. fallible
7. fragment
8. elaborate
9. fauna
10. froth
11. ecstasy
12. emulate

PAGE 95
Sentences will vary, but confirm that assigned word has been used properly.

PAGE 96
1. grimace
2. goblet
3. genuflect
4. homage
5. headquarters
6. hearth
7. grandiose
8. gallant
9. heritage
10. harvest
11. garment

PAGE 97
Answers will vary. Check students' sentences for correct use of the words.

PAGE 98
1. jaguar
2. illusion
3. inexpensive
4. jiggle
5. jungle
6. jumbo
7. jargon
8. identical
9. inconsistent
10. juvenile
11. inhale

PAGE 99
Answers will vary. Check students' sentences for correct use of the words.

PAGE 100
1. literacy
2. kernel
3. leisure
4. kiosk
5. lacquer
6. lopsided
7. kaleidoscope
8. languid
9. kosher
10. keg
11. kindle

PAGE 101
Answers will vary. Check students' sentences for correct use of the words.

PAGE 102
1. martyr
2. nomadic
3. naive
4. modem
5. muffin
6. nudge
7. nozzle
8. Mildew
9. mahogany
10. menace
11. nonchalant
12. necessary

PAGE 103
Answers will vary. Check students' sentences for correct use of the words.

PAGE 104
1. posture
2. patriarch
3. octave
4. pedicure
5. omnivorous
6. ordeal
7. obituary
8. purpose
9. ottoman
10. prize
11. phantom
12. original

PAGE 105
Answers will vary. Check students' sentences for correct use of the words.

PAGE 106
1. repent
2. quince
3. quell
4. quad
5. redeem
6. quota
7. rampage
8. quake
9. reverse
10. queasy
11. rupture

PAGE 107
Answers will vary. Check students' sentences for correct use of the words.

PAGE 108
1. temerity
2. tactful
3. triceps
4. sacrifice
5. smear
6. stiff
7. temper
8. silhouette
9. swelter
10. spare
11. thorn
12. segment

PAGE 109
Answers will vary. Check students' sentences for correct use of the words.

PAGE 110
1. varnish
2. unaccompanied
3. unkempt
4. ulcer
5. vulgar
6. vivid
7. undisciplined
8. vicinity
9. unsound
10. valid
11. utter

PAGE 111
Answers will vary. Check students' sentences for correct use of the words.

PAGE 112
1. whiff
2. X-axis
3. xerothermic
4. xenophobe
5. wharf
6. wad
7. wade
8. Xylem
9. xerography
10. wallet
11. warble

PAGE 113
Answers will vary. Check students' sentences for correct use of the words.

PAGE 114
1. yogurt
2. yearling
3. yoga
4. yacht
5. yam
6. zodiac
7. zealot
8. yelp
9. zenith
10. zori
11. zinnia

PAGE 115
Answers will vary. Check students' sentences for correct use of the words.

PAGE 116
1. because a *fakir* is a Hindu or Muslim holy person who is a beggar, and a *fedora* is a hat that such a beggar would not be able to afford
2. at its *perigee* because then the moon is closest to the earth
3. because an *ascetic* is someone who has chosen not to have pleasure or comforts, and *silk* is a luxury cloth
4. because a *buccaneer* is a pirate and a *brigantine* is a type of ship

5. because an *impostor* would be hiding his identity, and going *incognito* would accomplish this purpose
6. *rhinestones*, because *lodestones* are naturally magnetized pieces of magnetite, an iron ore, not a stone used in jewelry
7. because a *semaphore* is a tower with movable arms used to signal railroad trains
8. a *jennet* because it is a small Spanish horse

PAGE 117
1. a *lectern* because a teacher often gives a lecture, and a lectern is a piece of furniture that can hold notes and a microphone, whereas *legerdemain* is the use of trickery or magic
2. *rectitude* because it is honesty and goodness in principles and conduct, whereas *iniquity* is great evil or injustice
3. a *bellicose* person because such a person would be likely to pick a fight, whereas a *comatose* person is in a coma
4. a *loquacious* person because such a person is talkative, whereas a *mendacious* person tells lies
5. an *adjustable* bed because such a bed can move up and down and bend to make the patient more comfortable; a bed would not be considered *reversible*
6. in an *agrarian* setting, because the *bobolink*, a bird, is more likely to be found in the country than in the city
7. a person who had *versatility* because such a person would be able to do many different tasks, whereas someone who had *culpability* would be guilty of some wrongdoing

PAGE 118
ACROSS:
2. compare
6. discount
9. ingredients
10. label
11. factory
12. comparison
13. sale
14. credit
16. exchange
17. cosmetics
18. guarantee

DOWN:
1. quality
3. pricetag
4. dry clean
5. lightweight
7. department
8. price
10. lingerie
15. large

PAGE 119
1. ingredients
2. factory
3. label
4. department
5. dry clean
6. discount
7. exchange
8. quality
9. cosmetics
10. credit
11. pricetag, price
12. sale

PAGE 120
ACROSS:
2. swear
6. jury
7. testify
9. parole
10. sentence
11. trial
14. summation
15. defendant
16. truth
17. argue
18. defense

DOWN:
1. plaintiff
3. witness
4. probation
5. prosecution
6. justice
8. verdict
12. attorney
13. judge

PAGE 121
1. witness
2. probation
3. verdict
4. trial
5. jury
6. prosecution
7. defendant
8. defense
9. prosecution
10. truth
11. judge
12. justice

PAGE 122
ACROSS:
1. permits
5. landscaping
6. irrigation
10. bulldozer
11. construction
12. drywall
14. foundation
15. architect

DOWN:
2. shingles
3. patio
4. electrician
7. plumber
8. concrete
9. contractor
13. blueprint

PAGE 123
1. landscaping
2. irrigation
3. shingles
4. blueprint
5. architect
6. patio
7. plumber
8. permits
9. concrete
10. electrician
11. Construction
12. contractor

PAGE 124
ACROSS:
2. propulsion
6. rocket
7. interstellar
8. astronaut
9. orbit
10. launch
12. infinity
14. moon
16. satellite
17. quarks

DOWN:
1. spacecraft
3. interplanetary
4. galaxy
5. gravity
11. cosmos
13. planet
15. pulsar

PAGE 125
1. astronaut
2. rocket
3. launch
4. orbit
5. gravity
6. galaxy
7. planet
8. moon
9. interstellar
10. Interplanetary
11. pulsar
12. quark

143

PAGE 126

ACROSS:
4. muscular
6. stress
9. vitamin
10. capillary
13. fiber
14. lipid
15. treatment
16. heartbeat

DOWN:
1. cardiovascular
2. nutrition
3. insomnia
4. mineral
5. carbohydrates
7. fatigue
8. metabolism
11. stretch
12. symptom

PAGE 127
1. vitamin
2. carbohydrates
3. muscular
4. nutrition
5. stretch
6. heartbeat
7. stress
8. fatigue
9. insomnia
10. symptom
11. metabolism
12. treatment

PAGE 128

ACROSS:
1. cubicle
4. assistant
7. client
8. employee
12. secretary
13. overtime
14. deadline
15. meeting

DOWN:
2. benefits
3. employer
5. salary
6. committee
7. conference
9. vacation
10. president
11. project

PAGE 129
1. vacation
2. client
3. committee
4. employee
5. project
6. deadline
7. employer
8. benefits
9. salary
10. overtime
11. secretary
12. president

PAGE 130

ACROSS:
1. tropical
3. safari
4. passport
7. restaurant
9. accommodations
12. hotel
13. sightseeing
15. pyramids
16. souvenir
17. translate

DOWN:
2. airfare
3. suitcase
5. transportation
6. security
8. photographs
10. museum
11. guide
14. tourist

PAGE 131
1. pyramids
2. transportation
3. passport
4. security
5. airfare
6. suitcase
7. hotel
8. sightseeing
9. translate
10. souvenir
11. photographs
12. safari

PAGE 132

ACROSS:
4. executive
6. preamble
7. amendments
9. judicial
11. Democrat
13. legislative
14. impeach
15. agency
16. cabinet

DOWN:
1. lobbyist
2. electoral
3. Republican
5. Constitution
8. Senate
10. decision
12. elect

PAGE 133
1. Constitution
2. amendments
3. judicial
4. executive
5. legislative
6. Senate
7. Democrat
8. Republican
9. preamble
10. cabinet
11. electoral
12. lobbyist
13. decisions

PAGE 134

ACROSS:
2. occasion
7. guests
8. gala
10. refreshments
13. entertainment
14. introduction
15. interaction
16. amusement

DOWN:
1. conversation
3. caterer
4. partner
5. celebration
6. banquet
9. appetizers
11. event
12. formal

PAGE 135
1. Refreshments
2. Formal
3. introduction
4. interaction or conversation
5. partner
6. occasion
7. guests
8. celebration
9. entertainment
10. banquet
11. appetizers
12. caterer